Marco Colombo

LPIC-1 101-500 Practice Exams

250 Questions and Answers to test your knowledge

2019

First Printing: 2019

ISBN: 978-0-244-46616-9

Contents

Acknowledgment

It's been about ten years since I wrote my last acknowledgments for "something" that I have done. Now that I think about it, it was almost twelve years ago. The thesis is a distant and pleasant memory and now, after many years, I have the opportunity to thank someone again.

I could do the usual list of names such as mom, dad, girlfriend, cousins, friends, relatives, explaining in detail how they helped me in writing this book. I could, but I would like to do something different. They already know how important they have been to me.

I would like to thank WHO has given me the opportunity to do all this, giving me health, idea and initiative in completing this work, believing I can do something good and useful, which had left intact my dearest loved ones, like 10 years ago, surrounding me with new people who make me feel loved every day (I apologize if I cannot do the same). Of course, I have also met negative people, but I think they have been put on my way to understand how I do not want to be.

Finally, a last thought goes to my uncle who is no longer with us and now, from there, with my grandparents, gives me the strength to work hard, to do things that I love and to reach new goals.

Preface

The Linux Professional Institute has developed a multi-level Linux professional certification program for people who deal with the Linux world. The LPIC-1 certification is the first certification in this program and, to become LPIC-1 certified, you must pass both the LPI 101 and LPI 102 exams. At the time of writing (February 2019) the Version is 5.0 and the Exam Codes are 101-500 and 102-500.

Through this book you have the opportunity to test your skills in preparing the LPI 101 exam. You can find the objectives of the exam, identified by the Linux Professional Institute, an assessment test to understand your entry level and four practice exams (questions and answers) to test your knowledge before taking the real exam.

The 250 questions are not the original questions of the exam, but they have been thought as useful exercises to focus on the main topics and to reinforce what you learned, improving your Linux skills. Each question is explained adequately, providing not only the correct answer, but also the general background to which the question refers.

Exam 101-500 Objectives

Topic 101: System Architecture

101.1 Determine and configure hardware settings (weight 2)

Description:

Candidates should be able to determine and configure fundamental system hardware.

Key Knowledge Areas:

- Enable and disable integrated peripherals

- Differentiate between the various types of mass storage devices

- Determine hardware resources for devices

- Tools and utilities to list various hardware information (e.g. lsusb, lspci, etc.)

- Tools and utilities to manipulate USB devices

- Conceptual understanding of sysfs, udev and dbus

Partial list of the used files, terms and utilities:

/sys/, /proc/, /dev/, modprobe, lsmod, lspci, lsusb

101.2 Boot the system (weight 3)

Description:

Candidates should be able to guide the system through the booting process.

Key Knowledge Areas:

- Provide common commands to the boot loader and options to the kernel at boot time

- Demonstrate knowledge of the boot sequence from BIOS/UEFI to boot completion

- Understanding of SysVinit and systemd

- Awareness of Upstart

- Check boot events in the log files

Partial list of the used files, terms and utilities:

dmesg, journalctl, BIOS, UEFI, bootloader, kernel, initramfs, init, SysVinit, systemd

101.3 Change runlevels / boot targets and shutdown or reboot system (weight 3)

Description:

Candidates should be able to manage the SysVinit runlevel or systemd boot target of the system. This objective includes changing to single user mode, shutdown or rebooting the system. Candidates should be able to alert users before switching runlevels / boot targets and properly terminate processes. This objective also includes setting the default SysVinit runlevel or systemd boot target. It also includes awareness of Upstart as an alternative to SysVinit or systemd.

Key Knowledge Areas:

- Set the default runlevel or boot target

- Change between runlevels / boot targets including single user mode.

- Shutdown and reboot from the command line

- Alert users before switching runlevels / boot targets or other major system events

- Properly terminate processes

- Awareness of acpid

Partial list of the used files, terms and utilities:

/etc/inittab, shutdown, init, /etc/init.d/, telinit, systemd, systemctl, /etc/systemd/, /usr/lib/systemd/, wall

Topic 102: Linux Installation and Package Management

102.1 Design hard disk layout (weight 2)

Description:

Candidates should be able to design a disk partitioning scheme for a Linux system.

Key Knowledge Areas:

- Allocate filesystems and swap space to separate partitions or disks

- Tailor the design to the intended use of the system

- Ensure the /boot partition conforms to the hardware architecture requirements for booting

- Knowledge of basic features of LVM

Partial list of the used files, terms and utilities:

/ (root) filesystem, /var filesystem, /home filesystem, /boot filesystem, EFI System Partition (ESP), swap space, mount points, partitions

102.2 Install a boot manager (weight 2)

Description:

Candidates should be able to select, install and configure a boot manager.

Key Knowledge Areas:

- Providing alternative boot locations and backup boot options

- Install and configure a boot loader such as GRUB Legacy

- Perform basic configuration changes for GRUB 2

- Interact with the boot loader

Partial list of the used files, terms and utilities:

menu.lst, grub.cfg and grub.conf, grub-install, grub-mkconfig, MBR

102.3 Manage shared libraries (weight 1)

Description:

Candidates should be able to determine the shared libraries that executable programs depend on and install them when necessary.

Key Knowledge Areas:

- Identify shared libraries
- Identify the typical locations of system libraries
- Load shared libraries

Partial list of the used files, terms and utilities:

ldd, ldconfig, /etc/ld.so.conf, LD_LIBRARY_PATH

102.4 Use Debian package management (weight 3)

Description:

Candidates should be able to perform package management using the Debian package tools.

Key Knowledge Areas:

- Install, upgrade and uninstall Debian binary packages
- Find packages containing specific files or libraries which may or may not be installed
- Obtain package information like version, content, dependencies, package integrity and installation status (whether or not the package is installed)
- Awareness of apt

Partial list of the used files, terms and utilities:

/etc/apt/sources.list, dpkg, dpkg-reconfigure, apt-get, apt-cache

102.5 Use RPM and YUM package management (weight 3)

Description:

Candidates should be able to perform package management using RPM, YUM and Zypper.

Key Knowledge Areas:

- Install, re-install, upgrade and remove packages using RPM, YUM and Zypper

- Obtain information on RPM packages such as version, status, dependencies, integrity and signatures

- Determine what files a package provides, as well as find which package a specific file comes from

- Awareness of dnf

Partial list of the used files, terms and utilities:

rpm, rpm2cpio, /etc/yum.conf, /etc/yum.repos.d/, yum, zypper

102.6 Linux as a virtualization guest (weight 1)

Description:

Candidates should understand the implications of virtualization and cloud computing on a Linux guest system.

Key Knowledge Areas:

- Understand the general concept of virtual machines and containers

- Understand common elements virtual machines in an IaaS cloud, such as computing instances, block storage and networking

- Understand unique properties of a Linux system which have to changed when a system is cloned or used as a template

- Understand how system images are used to deploy virtual machines, cloud instances and containers

- Understand Linux extensions which integrate Linux with a virtualization product

- Awareness of cloud-init

Partial list of the used files, terms and utilities:

Virtual machine, Linux container, Application container, Guest drivers, SSH host keys, D-Bus machine id

Topic 103: GNU and Unix Commands

103.1 Work on the command line (weight 4)

Description:

Candidates should be able to interact with shells and commands using the command line. The objective assumes the Bash shell.

Key Knowledge Areas:

- Use single shell commands and one-line command sequences to perform basic tasks on the command line
- Use and modify the shell environment including defining, referencing and exporting environment variables
- Use and edit command history
- Invoke commands inside and outside the defined path

Partial list of the used files, terms and utilities:

bash, echo, env, export, pwd, set, unset, type, which, man, uname, history, .bash_history, Quoting

103.2 Process text streams using filters (weight 2)

Description:

Candidates should be able to apply filters to text streams.

Key Knowledge Areas:

- Send text files and output streams through text utility filters to modify the output using standard UNIX commands found in the GNU textutils package

Partial list of the used files, terms and utilities:

bzcat, cat, cut, head, less, md5sum, nl, od, paste, sed, sha256sum, sha512sum, sort, split, tail, tr, uniq, wc, xzcat, zcat

103.3 Perform basic file management (weight 4)

Description:

Candidates should be able to use the basic Linux commands to manage files and directories.

Key Knowledge Areas:

- Copy, move and remove files and directories individually
- Copy multiple files and directories recursively
- Remove files and directories recursively
- Use simple and advanced wildcard specifications in commands
- Using find to locate and act on files based on type, size, or time
- Usage of tar, cpio and dd

Partial list of the used files, terms and utilities:

cp, find, mkdir, mv, ls, rm, rmdir, touch, tar, cpio, dd, file, gzip, gunzip, bzip2, bunzip2, xz, unxz, file globbing

103.4 Use streams, pipes and redirects (weight 4)

Description:

Candidates should be able to redirect streams and connect them in order to efficiently process textual data. Tasks include redirecting standard input, standard output and standard error, piping the output of one command to the input of another command, using the output of one command as arguments to another command and sending output to both stdout and a file.

Key Knowledge Areas:

- Redirecting standard input, standard output and standard error
- Pipe the output of one command to the input of another command
- Use the output of one command as arguments to another command
- Send output to both stdout and a file

Partial list of the used files, terms and utilities:

tee, xargs

103.5 Create, monitor and kill processes (weight 4)

Description:

Candidates should be able to perform basic process management.

Key Knowledge Areas:

- Run jobs in the foreground and background
- Signal a program to continue running after logout
- Monitor active processes
- Select and sort processes for display
- Send signals to processes

Partial list of the used files, terms and utilities:

&, bg, fg, jobs, kill, nohup, ps, top, free, uptime, pgrep, pkill, killall, watch, screen, tmux

103.6 Modify process execution priorities (weight 2)

Description:

Candidates should be able to manage process execution priorities.

Key Knowledge Areas:

- Know the default priority of a job that is created
- Run a program with higher or lower priority than the default
- Change the priority of a running process

Partial list of the used files, terms and utilities:

nice, ps, renice, top

103.7 Search text files using regular expressions (weight 3)

Description:

Candidates should be able to manipulate files and text data using regular expressions. This objective includes creating simple regular expressions containing several notational elements as well as understanding the differences between basic and extended regular expressions. It also includes using regular expression tools to perform searches through a filesystem or file content.

Key Knowledge Areas:

- Create simple regular expressions containing several notational elements

- Understand the differences between basic and extended regular expressions

- Understand the concepts of special characters, character classes, quantifiers and anchors

- Use regular expression tools to perform searches through a filesystem or file content

- Use regular expressions to delete, change and substitute text

Partial list of the used files, terms and utilities:

grep, egrep, fgrep, sed, regex(7)

103.8 Basic file editing (weight 3)

Description:

Candidates should be able to edit text files using vi. This objective includes vi navigation, vi modes, inserting, editing, deleting, copying and finding text. It also includes awareness of other common editors and setting the default editor.

Key Knowledge Areas:

- Navigate a document using vi

- Understand and use vi modes

- Insert, edit, delete, copy and find text in vi

- Awareness of Emacs, nano and vim
- Configure the standard editor

Partial list of the used files, terms and utilities:

vi, /, ?, h ,j, k, l, i, o, a, d, p, y, dd, yy, ZZ, :w!, :q!, EDITOR

Topic 104: Devices, Linux Filesystems, Filesystem Hierarchy Standard

104.1 Create partitions and filesystems (weight 2)

Description:

Candidates should be able to configure disk partitions and then create filesystems on media such as hard disks. This includes the handling of swap partitions.

Key Knowledge Areas:

- Manage MBR and GPT partition tables

- Use various mkfs commands to create various filesystems such as ext2/ext3/ext4, XFS, VFAT, exFAT

- Basic feature knowledge of Btrfs, including multi-device filesystems, compression and subvolumes

Partial list of the used files, terms and utilities:

fdisk, gdisk, parted, mkfs, mkswap

104.2 Maintain the integrity of filesystems (weight 2)

Description:

Candidates should be able to maintain a standard filesystem, as well as the extra data associated with a journaling filesystem.

Key Knowledge Areas:

- Verify the integrity of filesystems

- Monitor free space and inodes

- Repair simple filesystem problems

Partial list of the used files, terms and utilities:

du, df, fsck, e2fsck, mke2fs, tune2fs, xfs_repair, xfs_fsr, xfs_db

104.3 Control mounting and unmounting of filesystems (weight 3)

Description:

Candidates should be able to configure the mounting of a filesystem.

Key Knowledge Areas:

- Manually mount and unmount filesystems
- Configure filesystem mounting on bootup
- Configure user mountable removable filesystems
- Use of labels and UUIDs for identifying and mounting file systems
- Awareness of systemd mount units

Partial list of the used files, terms and utilities:

/etc/fstab, /media/, mount, umount, blkid, lsblk

104.4 Removed

104.5 Manage file permissions and ownership (weight 3)

Description:

Candidates should be able to control file access through the proper use of permissions and ownerships.

Key Knowledge Areas:

- Manage access permissions on regular and special files as well as directories
- Use access modes such as suid, sgid and the sticky bit to maintain security
- Know how to change the file creation mask

- Use the group field to grant file access to group members

Partial list of the used files, terms and utilities:

chmod, umask, chown, chgrp

104.6 Create and change hard and symbolic links (weight 2)

Description:

Candidates should be able to create and manage hard and symbolic links to a file.

Key Knowledge Areas:

- Create links
- Identify hard and/or soft links
- Copying versus linking files
- Use links to support system administration tasks

Partial list of the used files, terms and utilities:

ln, ls

104.7 Find system files and place files in the correct location (weight 2)

Description:

Candidates should be thoroughly familiar with the Filesystem Hierarchy Standard (FHS), including typical file locations and directory classifications.

Key Knowledge Areas:

- Understand the correct locations of files under the FHS
- Find files and commands on a Linux system
- Know the location and purpose of important file and directories as defined in the FHS

Partial list of the used files, terms and utilities:

find, locate, updatedb, whereis, which, type, /etc/updatedb.conf

Assessment Test

1. You want to display the username, hostname and current working directory in your default bash prompt, making it more meaning full. Which of the following shell variables do you need to edit?

    A. BASH_PROMPT

    B. TERM

    C. DEFAULT_PROMPT

    D. PS1

2. What is the effect of the following command?

```
echo $(date) >> datetime
```

    A. If a shell variable named **date** exists, its value is appended to the **datetime** file, otherwise you get an error message

    B. The current system date and time is appended to the **datetime** file

    C. The **date** string is appended to the **datetime** file

    D. If a shell variable named **date** exists, its value is appended to the **datetime** file, otherwise a blank line is appended

    E. It assigns the current system date and time (as a string value) to the **datetime** variable

3. Your Linux system has five partitions on a MBR formatted disk: **/dev/sda1**, **/dev/sda2**, **/dev/sda5**, **/dev/sda6** and **/dev/sda7**. Which of the following statements is true?

   A. The disk contains two primary partitions, one extended partition and two logical partitions

   B. The disk contains one primary partition, one extended partition and three logical partitions

   C. The disk contains two primary partitions and three extended partitions

   D. The disk contains two logical partitions and three primary partitions

   E. It is not a valid scheme: you should have: **/dev/sda1**, **/dev/sda2**, **/dev/sda3**, **/dev/sda4** and **/dev/sda5**

4. You want to set up a Linux swap area on the device named **/dev/sda2**. Which of the following commands can you use? Assume you are acting as root.

   A. swap2fs /dev/sda2

   B. mkfs.swap /dev/sda2

   C. mkswap /dev/sda2

   D. mke2swap /dev/sda2

5. Using **yum**, you want to check if updates for your packages are available by displaying their names, version and repository area. Which of the following commands can you use?

   A. yum update

   B. yum check-update

   C. yum show-updates

   D. yum search available-updates

6. You want to create a hard link named **foo** to the **bar** file. Which of the following commands can you use? Select two.

   A. ln -s bar foo

   B. ln bar foo

   C. cp -l bar foo

   D. cp -s bar foo

   E. hlink bar foo

7. What signal do you need to send to a process so that it can orderly shutdown, for example, closing open files before exiting? What is its matching number?

   A. SIGTERM (15)

   B. SIGKILL (9)

   C. SIGSOFT (9)

   D. SIGSTOP (19)

   E. SIGEXIT (15)

8. You want to move the **/home/foo/script** directory and all its files and subdirectories under the **/home/foo/customizations** directory. Which of the following commands can you use? Assume you are acting as system administrator.

   A. mv -r ~foo/script/ ~foo/customizations/

   B. mv -R ~foo/script/ ~foo/customizations/

   C. mv ~foo/script/ ~foo/customizations/

   D. mv --recursive ~foo/script/ ~foo/customizations/

9. You want to know the number of lines of the **employees.txt** and **facilities.txt** files and the total count of lines (the sum of lines of both files). Which of the following commands can you use? Assume that these two files exist in your current working directory.

   A. count -l employees.txt facilities.txt

   B. wc -l employees.txt facilities.txt

   C. nl employees.txt facilities.txt

   D. You cannot perform this operation

10. Which of the following sequences better describes the traditional boot process for a BIOS-based Linux system?

   A. BIOS - kernel - boot loader - /sbin/init

   B. BIOS - boot loader - GUI

   C. boot loader - BIOS - kernel - /sbin/init

   D. BIOS - boot loader - kernel - /sbin/init

   E. boot loader - BIOS - /sbin/init - kernel

   F. BIOS - kernel - GUI

Answers to the Assessment Test

1. **D - Topic103.1**

The **PS1** shell variable represents the default prompt in bash. So, if you want to customize your bash prompt, making it more meaning full, you need to edit this variable. In particular, you can change the value of **PS1** to **\u \h \w** to display the username, hostname and full path of the current working directory. Therefore, option D is the correct answer. The **TERM** variable specifies the type of the running terminal and so option B is incorrect. In bash the BASH_PROMPT and DEFAULT_PROMPT variables do not exist by default, making options A and C incorrect.

2. **B - Topic 103.4**

The question shows an example of command substitution that is used to allow the output of a command to replace the command itself. It occurs when a command is enclosed as follows: **$(command)** or `` `command` ``. So the output of the **date** command (that is the system date and time) replaces the command itself and is appended, trough the **>>** redirection operator, to the **datetime** file. This makes option B the correct answer.

3. **B - Topic 102.1**

The MBR partitioning system uses up to four primary partitions, numbered from one to four, one of which can be an extended partition. The extended partition is a special type of primary partition that contains logical partitions that are numbered five and up. So the partition scheme of the question is valid and, according to this, you have one primary partition (either **/dev/sda1** or

/dev/sda2), one extended partition (either **/dev/sda1** or **/dev/sda2**) and three logical partitions (**/dev/sda5**, **/dev/sda6** and **/dev/sda7**). This makes option B the correct answer.

4. C - Topic 104.1

The **mkswap** command is used to set up a Linux swap area on a device or in a file. Once you have created the swap area, you must activate it with the **swapon** command. Therefore, option C is the correct answer.

5. B - Topic 102.5

Yum is an interactive, rpm based, package manager. It has several subcommands such as **check-update** that is used to check if updates for your packages are available. Therefore, option B is the correct answer. The command in option A is used to update every currently installed package, while the command in option D is used to search package names, summaries, packagers and descriptions for the **available-updates** keyword and so these options are incorrect. Finally, option C contains an invalid subcommand and is therefore incorrect.

6. B, C - Topic 104.6

Hard links are directory entries that point to the same inode. In order to create hard links, you can use the **ln** command or the **cp** command with the -l (--link) option. Therefore, options B and C are the correct answers. The **ln** command with the -s (--symbolic) option is used to make symbolic links instead of hard links, while the **cp** command with the -s (--symbolic-link) option is used to make symbolic links instead of copying. This makes options A and D incorrect. Option E contains an invalid command and is therefore incorrect.

7. A - Topic 103.5

In Linux you can use the **kill -l** command to list available signals, each of which has a name and a number. The SIGTERM signal has a numerical value of 15 and it causes a process to orderly shutdown, for example, cleaning up or closing open files before exiting. The SIGKILL signal has a numerical value of 9 and it causes a process to exit without performing a tidy cleanup and shutdown. The SIGSTOP signal has a numerical value of 19 and it instructs the operating system to stop a process for later resumption. The SIGSOFT and SIGEXIT signals are not valid. Therefore, option A is the correct answer.

8. C - Topic 103.3

The **mv** command is used to move or rename files. In order to access to the home directory of the **foo** user, you can use the **~foo** syntax. In fact, the shell replaces it transparently with the home directory of **foo** and passes that in its place. So, to move the specified directory and its files and subdirectories under another directory, you can use the command shown in option C that is the therefore the correct answer. For completeness, the **mv** command has not the -r, -R and --recursive options indicated in options A, B and D.

9. B - Topic 103.2

The **wc** command is used to print newline, word, and byte counts for each file specified on the command line and a total line if more than one file is indicated. You can use the -c (--bytes) option to print the byte counts, the -m (--chars) option to print the character counts, the -l (--lines) option to print the newline counts, the -L (--max-line-length) option to print the length of the longest line and the -w (--words) option to print the word counts. Therefore, option B is the correct answer, while option D is incorrect. The **nl** command is used to write each specified file to standard output with line numbers added and so option C is incorrect. The **count** command is not valid and this makes option A the incorrect answer.

10. D - Topic 101.2

Option D describes the traditional boot process for a BIOS-based Linux system correctly. In fact, when a PC is turned on or rebooted the BIOS searches, loads and executes a boot loader and the boot loader loads and executes a secondary boot loader (optional) and the kernel. Then the kernel loads and executes /sbin/init that is responsible for starting the rest of the system services on a Linux machine.

101-500
Practice Exams

Practice Exam 1

1. You want to print the full pathname of your current working directory to find out if you are in the exact location to launch (just typing its name) a custom application named **foo** that is not in your **$PATH**. Which of the following commands can you use? Select two.

    A. echo WORKING_DIR

    B. pwd

    C. cat cwd

    D. echo $WD

    E. echo $PWD

2. What's the difference between typing **I** or **A** when you are using the **vi** editor? Assume **vi** is in command mode.

    A. **I** will enter insert mode after the character at the current position, while **A** will enter insert mode before the character at the current position

    B. **I** will enter insert mode before the character at the current position, while **A** will enter insert mode after the character at the current position

    C. **I** will enter insert mode at the beginning of the current line, while **A** will enter insert mode at the end of the current line

    D. **I** will enter insert mode at the end of the current line, while **A** will enter insert mode at the beginning of the current line

3. You want to set the ownership of the **foo** file to the user named **barusr**. Which of the following commands can you use? Assume you have root privileges.

    A. You cannot perform this operation

    B. chmod barusr foo

    C. chown barusr foo

    D. chgrp barusr foo

4. In the bash shell you type:

```
cat view.txt 2>&1 >report.txt
```

What is the result? Assume that the **view.txt** file does not exist.

    A. An empty file named **view.txt** is created

    B. An error message is printed on the terminal and also written in the **report.txt** file

    C. An error message is written in the **report.txt** file

    D. An error message is printed on the terminal and an empty file named **report.txt** is created

5. You want to locate the full pathname of the executable file that will be run when you type **date** on the command line. Which of the following commands can you use?

    A. which date

    B. locate date

    C. lookup date

    D. search date

6. You want to review some kernel messages on your system. Which of the following commands can you use to examine the so called kernel ring buffer?

    A. cat /var/log/messages

    B. cat /var/log/messages | grep *boot*

    C. kmesg

    D. dmesg

7. You want to install a specific package, but you remember only the first part of its complex and very long name. Which of the following commands can you use to do keyword-based package searches on a Debian derived GNU/Linux system?

    A. apt-cache locate

    B. apt-cache find

    C. apt-cache search

    D. apt-cache query

8. Working with bash, you want to delete the shell variables named **var_foobar** and **var_barfoo** that you have mistakenly created. Which command can you use to accomplish this task? Write only the command name.

9. You have a file named **employees.txt** with three columns: Name, Surname, Identification Number. You want to sort this file using the Surname field as sort field, deleting duplicated lines. Which of the following commands can you use?

    A. sort -k2 employees.txt | uniq -d

    B. sort -k2 employees.txt | uniq

    C. sort employees.txt | uniq

    D. uniq employees.txt

10. You want to print the value of the **SHELL** environment variable to the standard output to see the full pathname of the current command shell. Which of the following commands can you use?

    A. echo $SHELL

    B. cat SHELL

    C. echo SHELL

    D. vi SHELL

11. You want to remove the file named **-file** that you have mistakenly created. Which of the following commands can you use?

    A. rm \-file

    B. rm "-file"

    C. rm '-file'

    D. rm -- -file

12. You want to read from standard input and write to standard output and to a file named **foobar**. Which command can you use? Write only the command name.

13. You want to test the effect of new experimental libraries before using them for all your programs. Which environment variable do you need to edit to specify the list of the additional directories where the new library files may be found?

    A. LIBRARY_PATH

    B. LD_PATH_LIBRARY

    C. PATH_LIBRARY

    D. LD_LIBRARY_PATH

14. Some directories can be split off into separate partitions, but others can't because they are vital for the boot process. According to the FHS, which of the following directories are common Linux partitions? Select two.

    A. /bin

    B. /sbin

    C. /boot

    D. /home

    E. /lib

15. You create a symbolic link **barfoo** to the file named **foobar** and then you accidentally delete the **foobar** file. Which of the following statements is true?

    A. You cannot delete a file if it has hard or symbolic links

    B. **barfoo** will become a broken link

    C. **barfoo** will be deleted

    D. **barfoo** will become a hard link

16. What is the effect of the following command?

```
foobar | xargs barfoo
```

    A. **foobar** is started with the output of **barfoo** as arguments

    B. **barfoo** is started with the output of **foobar** as arguments

    C. **foobar** and **barfoo** are started by the **xargs** command

    D. The output of the **foobar** command is appended to the **xargs** and **barfoo** files

17. Which file on Debian-based systems specifies locations (for example CD-ROM, local file system, HTTP, FTP) from which packages can be obtained? Write the full path.

18. You want to know the package that owns a file named **barfoo**. Which of the following commands can you use? Assume you are working with a RPM-based distribution.

    A. rpm -ql barfoo

    B. rpm -U barfoo

    C. rpm -qf barfoo

    D. rpm -qi barfoo

    E. rpm -F barfoo

19. You want to know the total space used by your **home** directory and all its subdirectories. Which of the following commands can you use?

    A. df -rk ~

    B. df -k ~

    C. du -k ~

    D. du -rk ~

20. Which of the following syntaxes can you use if you want to run three commands in sequence regardless of the success of the previous command?

    A. command1 && command2 && command3

    B. command1 || command2 || command3

    C. command1, command2, command3

    D. command1; command2; command3

21. Using bash, what is the effect of the following command?

```
barfoo &
```

    A. The **barfoo** command is started in foreground

    B. The **barfoo** command is started in background

    C. The **barfoo** command is suspended

    D. It is not a valid command

22. The **bar** user creates a program named **foo**. What is the maximum nice value that this ordinary user can set for **foo** when he uses the **nice** command?

    A. 19

    B. -19

    C. 20

    D. -20

23. Which of the following boot parameters do you have to pass to the kernel from the boot loader to set the initial command to be executed by the kernel (for example to boot to shell)?

    A. root

    B. init

    C. init_command

    D. bootinit

24. Using GRUB 2, you have just edited the **/etc/default/grub** file and now you want to generate the new configuration file. Which command can you use? Write only the command name.

25. Giving the following:

```
$jobs

[1] -  Stopped   xeyes

[2]    Running   xcalc &

[3] +  Stopped   ./script/script.sh

[4]    Running   xclock &
```

Using bash, how can you bring and execute the **xeyes** application in foreground?

A. bg %1

B. fg %1

C. bg %2

D. fg %2

E. Use CTRL+Z to switch trough the job list

26. What is the effect of the following command?

```
sed 's/foobar/barfoo/g' file.txt
```

A. It replaces all occurrences of **foobar** on each line with **barfoo** and overwrites the **file.txt** file

B. It replaces all occurrences of **foobar** on each line with **barfoo** and sends the modified text to the standard output

C. It replaces the first occurrence of **foobar** on each line with **barfoo** and overwrites the **file.txt** file

D. It replaces the first occurrence of **foobar** on each line with **barfoo** and sends the modified text to the standard output

E. It is not a valid command

27. Using **vi** in command mode, you press **pp**. What will be the result?

    A. The lines in the buffer will be put into the text after the current line twice

    B. The entire current line will be copied into the buffer

    C. The entire current line will be deleted

    D. The character under the cursor will be deleted

28. What is the effect of the following command?

```
kill 9 15
```

    A. It sends the **TERM** signal to the process with PID **15**

    B. It sends the **KILL** signal to the process with PID **15**

    C. It sends the **TERM** signal to the processes with PID **9** and **15**

    D. It sends the **KILL** signal to the processes with PID **9** and **15**

    E. It is an invalid command; you must specify which signal to send to your processes through the -s option

29. You want to reboot your System V-based system after a kernel update. Which of the following commands can you use? Assume you are acting as root. Select three.

    A. shutdown -r now

    B. shutdown --reboot now

    C. init 0

    D. init 6

    E. reboot

    F. restart

30. Which of the following commands can you use to create an archive file and to restore files from such an archive? Select two.

    A. gzip

    B. bzip2

    C. cpio

    D. tar

    E. archfile

31. Using System V, in which directory can you find the scripts used by **init** when starting the system, changing runlevels or shutting down?

    A. /etc/init.d

    B. /etc/system/init

    C. /etc/init/system.d

    D. /etc/runlevel.d

    E. /etc/runlevel/rc.d

32. Which of the following commands can you use to start the **Apache server**? Assume you are acting as root and your Debian system uses Systemd as system and service manager.

    A. /etc/init.d/apache2 start

    B. systemctl start apache2.service

    C. service start apache2

    D. systemctl apache2.service start

33. You want to know if the module named **foobar** is currently loaded in the kernel, also showing the other modules that depend on it. Which of the following commands can you use?

    A. mod | grep foobar

    B. lsmodule | grep foobar

    C. lsmod | grep foobar

    D. module | grep foobar

34. What is the result of the following command?

```
echo 'hello world' | tr A-Z a-z
```

    A. hello world

    B. HELLO WORLD

    C. Hello World

    D. It gives a syntax error

35. You are writing a text using the **vi** editor and you decide to save the edits you made. Which of the following combination keys do you have to press in order to switch to command mode and save the edits, leaving **vi** running and your file open?

    A. First press **CTRL**, then type **ZZ** and press Return

    B. First press **ESC**, then type **:wq** and press Return

    C. First press **ALT**, then type **:w** and press Return

    D. First press **ESC**, then type **:w** and press Return

    E. First press **TAB**, then type **:wq** and press Return

36. Which of the following commands is used by the system boot process to check the root filesystem and any other filesystem specified for checking in the **/etc/fstab** file?

    A. fsck -A

    B. fsrepair -a

    C. xfs_repair --all

    D. fsck_xfs -a

37. What's the difference between the **+** and ***** meta-characters in regular expressions?

    A. **+** indicates zero or more occurrences of the matching item, while ***** indicates zero or one occurrence of the matching item

    B. **+** indicates zero or one occurrence of the matching item, while ***** indicates one or more occurrences of the matching item

    C. **+** indicates zero or more occurrences of the matching item, while ***** indicates one or more occurrences of the matching item

    D. **+** indicates one or more occurrences of the matching item, while ***** indicates zero or more occurrences of the matching item

38. You have just set up a Linux swap area through **mkswap** and now you want to activate it. Which command, used to enable devices for paging and swapping, do you need to run?

    A. swap_activate

    B. swapon

    C. swapactivate

    D. swap_enable

39. Which of the following statements about the **lspci** command are false? Select two.

    A. With the **-nn** option it can be used to show PCI vendor and device codes as both numbers and names

    B. With the **-s** option it can be used to show only devices with specified vendor and device ID

    C. With the **-b** option it can be used to show all IRQ numbers and addresses as seen by the cards on the PCI bus instead of as seen by the kernel

    D. With the **-v** option it can be used to show a verbose output, reporting information such as the MAC address of the Ethernet network card

    E. With the **-t** option it can be used to show a tree-like diagram containing all buses, bridges, devices and connections between them

40. Using the **mkdir** command, you want to create multiple levels of subdirectories in a single command. Which of the following options can you use?

    A. -m

    B. -r

    C. -p

    D. -a

41. You want to list the installed files associated with the **pkg_bar** package. Which of the following commands can you use on a Debian derived GNU/Linux system?

    A. dpkg -S pkg_bar

    B. dpkg -L pkg_bar

    C. dpkg -C pkg_bar

    D. dpkg -l pkg_bar

42. You want to display all uncommented lines of the **/etc/network/interfaces** file. Which of the following commands can you use?

    A. grep '^#' /etc/network/interfaces

    B. grep -v '^$' /etc/network/interfaces

    C. grep -v '^#' /etc/network/interfaces

    D. grep '^[#]' /etc/network/interfaces

43. What's the meaning of the following command?

```
find . -size +100c -type f
```

    A. It finds all regular files in the current directory larger than 100 bytes in size

    B. It finds all regular files in the current directory of 100 bytes in size

    C. It finds all regular files in the current directory and in all subdirectories of 100 bytes in size

    D. It finds all regular files in the current directory and in all subdirectories larger than 100 bytes in size

44. You mounted a USB drive on your system, but you don't remember its mount point and its mount options. Which of the following commands can you use to list all mounted filesystems so that you can retrieve the information you need? Select two.

    A. cat /etc/fstab

    B. cat /proc/mounts

    C. mount -l

    D. mounts -l

    E. lsfs

45. You want to monitor the amount of free and used memory in the system, printing the output every 2 seconds. Which of the following commands can you use?

    A. uptime

    B. screen

    C. watch free

    D. tmux

46. Which of the following statements about GRUB Legacy and GRUB 2 are true? Select two.

    A. In GRUB 2 partitions and disks are numbered starting from 1 instead of 0 as happens in GRUB Legacy

    B. In GRUB 2 partitions are numbered starting from 1 instead of 0 as happens in GRUB Legacy

    C. In GRUB 2 disks are numbered starting from 1 instead of 0 as happens in GRUB Legacy

    D. GRUB 2 can boot an operating system from a LVM or RAID disk while GRUB Legacy can't

    E. GRUB 2 can also boot Windows Operating System while Grub Legacy can't

47. You have previously installed the **pkgfoobar** package on your system, but now you want to remove it. Which of the following commands can you use? Assume you are working with a RPM-based distribution.

    A. rpm -r pkgfoobar

    B. rpm -e pkgfoobar

    C. rpm --delete pkgfoobar

    D. rpm --cancel pkgfoobar

48. According to the FHS, which of the following directories contain a wealth of documentation such as the documentation written by developers or package maintainers?

    A. /usr/share/documentation

    B. /usr/share/docs

    C. /usr/share/doc

    D. /usr/doc

    E. /usr/docinfo

49. You have a Linux system with GRUB installed and you want to erase the entire MBR of the **/dev/sdb** device (thus also removing the partition table and the disk signature). Which of the following commands can you use?

    A. grub-remove /dev/sdb

    B. grub-install --erase /dev/sdb

    C. dd if=/dev/zero of=/dev/sdb bs=440 count=1

    D. dd if=/dev/zero of=/dev/sdb bs=512 count=1

50. Which of the following statements about virtual machines is true?

    A. Virtual machines can run on the same physical server only if they have the same operating system

    B. Each virtual machine runs a unique guest operating system

    C. Each virtual machine shares only the host operating system kernel

    D. Each virtual machine shares the host operating system kernel, the libraries and the binaries

51. You want to configure a system that uses **yum** to access additional **yum repositories**. In which directory do you have to put additional configuration files, each of which describes a new **yum repository** you want to access, to accomplish this task?

    A. /etc/yum/repository/repos.d

    B. /etc/yum/repos/repository.d

    C. /etc/yum.repos.d

    D. /etc/yum/package-files.d

52. Which of the following statements about MBR disks is true?

    A. MBR disks can hold at most one primary partition

    B. MBR disks can hold at most two primary partitions

    C. MBR disks can hold at most three primary partitions

    D. MBR disks can hold at most four primary partitions

53. You want to run the **foo** program, which uses a lot of CPU and takes a long time to finish its work, with a very low scheduling priority. Which command can you use? Write only the command name.

54. The **/dev/sda2** device is mounted on **/mnt/foo**. Which of the following commands can you use to unmount it?

    A. mount -u /mnt/foo

    B. umount /mnt/foo

    C. unmount /dev/sda2

    D. unmount /mnt/foo

55. Which of the following statements about UEFI booting is true?

    A. In UEFI booting the firmware executes the kernel directly to speed up the boot process

    B. In UEFI booting the firmware executes **/sbin/init** that then launches the boot loader that can help you set the boot order

    C. In UEFI booting the firmware executes a boot loader that then launches **/sbin/init** directly to speed up the boot process

    D. In UEFI booting the firmware executes a boot manager that can help you select which boot loader to launch

56. What's the meaning of the third field in the **/etc/fstab** file?

    A. The mount options associated with the filesystem

    B. The mount point for the filesystem

    C. The block special device or the remote filesystem to be mounted

    D. The type of the filesystem

    E. The filesystem check order

57. Typing **umask** in the bash shell gives the value of **0022**. Which default permissions match this **umask** value?

    A. 644 for files and 775 for directories

    B. 644 for files and 755 for directories

    C. 666 for files and 777 for directories

    D. 600 for files and 700 for directories

    E. 640 for files and 750 for directories

58. The **foo** user wants to set the file mode creation mask of his current shell execution environment to the value of 027. Which of the following commands can he use?

    A. He can't. Only the root user can perform this operation

    B. umask 027

    C. umask 750

    D. umask 640

59. What is the effect of the following command?

```
ln file2 file1
```

    A. It creates a hard link **file1** to **file2**

    B. It creates a hard link **file2** to **file1**

    C. It creates a symbolic link **file1** to **file2**

    D. It creates a symbolic link **file2** to **file1**

60. Using bash, you want to append the output of the **whoami** command to the **out.txt** file that is located in your current working directory. Which of the following commands can you use?

    A. whoami >> out.txt

    B. whoami > out.txt

    C. whoami | out.txt

    D. whoami &> out.txt

Practice Exam 2

1. In the bash shell you type:

```
cat view.txt >report.txt 2>&1
```

   What is the result? Assume that the **view.txt** file does not exist.

   A. An empty file named **view.txt** is created

   B. An error message is printed on the terminal and also written in the **report.txt** file

   C. An error message is written in the **report.txt** file

   D. An error message is printed on the terminal and an empty file named **report.txt** is created

2. According to the FHS, in which directory can you usually find the manual pages used by the **man** command? Write the full path.

3. You want to list all the installed packages on a Debian derived GNU/Linux system, also showing their version and a brief description. Which of the following commands can you use?

   A. dpkg -L

   B. dpkg -S

   C. dpkg -l

   D. dpkg -C

4. In bash you insert **2>&1** after the **foobar** command. What does it mean?

    A. It redirects the standard output to the current location of the standard error

    B. It redirects the standard error to the current location of the standard output

    C. It redirects the standard error to the current location of the standard input

    D. It redirects the standard input to the current location of the standard error

    E. It redirects the standard output to the current location of the standard input

5. What are the two (most favorable and least favorable) **nice** values that correspond to the highest and lowest scheduling priority for a process?

    A. 19 (highest scheduling priority) and -20 (lowest scheduling priority)

    B. -19 (highest scheduling priority) and 20 (lowest scheduling priority)

    C. 20 (highest scheduling priority) and -20 (lowest scheduling priority)

    D. -20 (highest scheduling priority) and 19 (lowest scheduling priority)

6. Output redirection using the **>** operator usually overwrites existing files, but you don't like this behavior. Which of the following commands can you type in the bash shell to change it, thus preventing accidental overwriting of existing files?

    A. set -o overwrite

    B. set -o owredir

    C. set -o owf

    D. set -o noclobber

7. You want to print the SHA512 (512-bit) checksum of the **foobar_image.iso** file. Which command can you use to accomplish this task? Write only the command name

8. You want to change some basic options in the **yum** main configuration file such as the debug message output level and the file name in which **yum** should write its logs. Which file do you need to edit?

    A. /etc/yum/repos.conf

    B. /etc/yum.conf

    C. /etc/yum.repos.conf

    D. /etc/repos/yum.repos.conf

9. Working with **vi**, you just finished to edit your text and now you want to save the changes you made and exit. Which of the following commands can you use to accomplish this task? Assume you have just pressed the ESC key and now **vi** is in command mode.

    A. :w

    B. :q!

    C. ZZ

    D. :!

10. Using GRUB 2, you want to change the **GRUB_TIMEOUT** variable and other general settings. Which file do you need to edit?

    A. /etc/grub/grub.conf

    B. /etc/grub.cfg

    C. /etc/grub.conf

    D. /etc/default/grub

11. You want to display detailed information about the **foobar** package. Which of the following commands can you use? Assume you are using **Zypper** as command line tool for package management in your OpenSUSE or SUSE Enterprise Linux platform.

    A. zypper show-info foobar

    B. zypper what-provides foobar

    C. zypper list-info foobar

    D. zypper info foobar

12. The **SIGHUP** signal is sent to a process when its controlling terminal is closed. What is its numerical value?

    A. 1

    B. 3

    C. 9

    D. 15

13. You want to add the **/foo** directory to the list of directories in which commands can be found so that you don't need to specify a fully qualified path each time you execute an application in this directory. Which environment variable do you need to edit? Write only the variable name.

14. You want to set the ownership of the **foo** file to the user named **barusr.** Which of the following commands can you use? Assume you have not root privileges.

    A. chown barusr foo

    B. chmod barusr foo

    C. You can set the ownership only if you are the file owner

    D. You cannot perform this operation

15. You want to display all the non-empty lines in the **/etc/network/interfaces** file. Which of the following commands can you use?

    A. grep '\.' /etc/network/interfaces

    B. grep -v '\.' /etc/network/interfaces

    C. grep '^$' /etc/network/interfaces

    D. grep -v '^$' /etc/network/interfaces

16. You have a set of library files in **/usr/local/lib** used by new custom applications and you want to add this directory to the library path for all users. What can you do to accomplish this task? Assume you are working as system administrator.

    A. Add the **/usr/local/lib** directory to **/etc/ld.so.conf** and then run **ldd**

    B. Add the **/usr/local/lib** directory to **/etc/ld.so.cache** and then run **ldd**

    C. Add the **/usr/local/lib** directory to **/etc/ld.so.cache** and then run **ldconfig**

    D. Add the **/usr/local/lib** directory to **/etc/ld.so.conf** and then run **ldconfig**

    E. Run the **ldd /usr/local/lib** command and then reboot the system

17. Which program is usually started as the first process of the system when the kernel finishes loading and what is its PID number?

    A. /sbin/init - PID 0

    B. /sbin/init - PID 1

    C. /usr/bin/startx - PID 0

    D. /usr/bin/startx - PID 1

18. You want to display the partitions on the MBR formatted disk named **/dev/sda** to see if an extended partition has already been created. Which of the following commands can you use? Assume you are acting with root privileges.

    A. mdisk -l /dev/sda

    B. partitions -l /dev/sda

    C. fdisk -l /dev/sda

    D. diskls -l /dev/sda

    E. lsdisk -l /dev/sda

19. What is the effect of the following command?

```
kill -9 15
```

    A. It sends the **TERM** signal to the process with PID **15**

    B. It sends the **QUIT** signal to the process with PID **15**

    C. It sends the **STOP** signal to the process with PID **15**

    D. It sends the **KILL** signal to the process with PID **15**

    E. It is an invalid command

20. You want to display the files contained in the uninstalled **pkgfoobar.rpm** package. Which of the following commands can you use? Assume you are working with a RPM-based distribution.

    A. rpm -ql pkgfoobar.rpm

    B. rpm -qi pkgfoobar.rpm

    C. rpm -qpl pkgfoobar.rpm

    D. rpm -Vf pkgfoobar.rpm

21. Which option of the **mke2fs** command specifies how the filesystem is going to be used so that **mke2fs** can choose optimal filesystem parameters for that use?

    A. -U

    B. -T

    C. -t

    D. -c

22. You have started the **foo** program, but you realize that it should run at a different priority. Which command can you use to alter the priority of this running program? Write only the command name.

23. You want to display the first 100 lines of the compressed file named **comp_file.gz**. Which of the following commands can you use?

    A. zcat comp_file.gz | head -100

    B. bzcat comp_file.gz | tail -100

    C. bzcat comp_file.gz | head -100

    D. xzcat comp_file.gz | tail -100

24. The ! prefix character can be used to recall a previous command from the history. What can you type in the command line to rerun the last command? Assume you are working with the bash shell.

    A. !2

    B. !-2

    C. !!

    D. !1

25. Some System V runlevels are reserved for special purposes. What are the numbers of these basic runlevels and what are their purposes?

    A. 0 (shut down the system) - 5 (multiuser mode with networking and X) - 6 (reboot the system)

    B. 0 (shut down the system) - 1 (single user mode) - 6 (reboot the system)

    C. 1 (single user mode) - 2 (multiuser mode without networking) - 3 (multiuser mode with networking)

    D. 1 (single user mode) - 2 (multiuser mode without networking) - 5 (multiuser mode with networking and X)

26. Which of the following boot parameters do you have to pass to the kernel from the boot loader to specify what device is to be used as the root filesystem while booting, thus overriding the root device of the system that the kernel was built on (the default value)?

    A. root

    B. fsroot

    C. rw

    D. rootfs

27. Which of the following options do you need to modify in your GRUB Legacy configuration file to specify which system to load if the user does not make a choice within a timeout?

    A. timeout

    B. root

    C. default

    D. kernel

28. Some directories can be split off into separate partitions, but others can't because they are vital for the boot process. According to the FHS, which of the following directories are not common Linux partitions? Select two.

    A. /etc

    B. /var

    C. /home

    D. /dev

    E. /usr

29. What is the effect of the following command?

```
ln -s file2 file1
```

    A. It creates a hard link **file1** to **file2**

    B. It creates a hard link **file2** to **file1**

    C. It creates a symbolic link **file1** to **file2**

    D. It creates a symbolic link **file2** to **file1**

30. You want to remove the **pkgfoobar** package on a Debian derived GNU/Linux system. Which of the following commands can you use? Select two.

    A. apt-get remove pkgfoobar

    B. apt-get delete pkgfoobar

    C. dpkg --remove pkgfoobar

    D. dpkg -d pkgfoobar

    E. dpkg --delete pkgfoobar

31. What's the meaning of the following command? Assume that all files and directories exist in the system.

```
cp /bar/foo /bar/foo1 /bar/foo2 /foo
```

    A. It copies the **/bar/foo**, **/bar/foo1**, **/bar/foo2** and **/foo** files to the current directory

    B. It copies the **/bar/foo**, **/bar/foo1** and **/bar/foo2** files to the **/foo** directory

    C. It copies the **/bar/foo** file to the **/bar/foo1**, **/bar/foo2** and **/foo** directories

    D. It is an invalid command and you get a syntax error

32. What is the effect of the following command?

```
mkfs /dev/sdc1
```

    A. It creates an **ext2** filesystem on **/dev/sdc1**

    B. It creates an **ext3** filesystem on **/dev/sdc1**

    C. It creates an **ext4** filesystem on **/dev/sdc1**

    D. It creates a **xfs** filesystem on **/dev/sdc1**

33. Working with **vi**, you want to copy the current line and the next 10 lines into the buffer. Which sequence of keys can you use to accomplish this task? Assume **vi** is in command mode.

    A. 11dd

    B. 11pp

    C. 11yy

    D. 11x

34. What are the Linux device filenames that correspond to the first and to the second serial port?

    A. **/dev/ttyS0** for the first serial port and **/dev/ttyS1** for the second serial port

    B. **/dev/ttyS1** for the first serial port and **/dev/ttyS2** for the second serial port

    C. **/dev/serial0** for the first serial port and **/dev/serial1** for the second serial port

    D. **/dev/serial1** for the first serial port and **/dev/serial2** for the second serial port

35. Which command do you have to run before installing or updating any package, and always after modifying **/etc/apt/sources.list** or adding files to **/etc/apt/sources.list.d** on a Debian derived GNU/Linux system?

    A. apt-get update

    B. apt-update

    C. apt-get updatedb

    D. updatedb

36. You want to set the permissions for a file so that it can be read and written by the owner and read by the group. Which of the following options contain the right octal value that you have to use with the **chmod** command?

    A. 640

    B. 644

    C. 600

    D. 700

37. Using System V, you want to switch from your graphical runlevel (multiuser mode with networking and X) to single user mode. Which of the following commands can you use? Assume you are acting as root. Select two.

    A. telinit 1

    B. shutdown -r single

    C. telinit s

    D. single

    E. telinit U

38. Which command can you use to change the group ownership of a file, but not the file owner? Write only the command name.

39. You have just unmounted your damaged **XFS** filesystem and now you want to attempt to repair it. Which of the following commands can you use?

    A. xfs_metadump

    B. repair_xfs

    C. xfs_repair

    D. clean_xfs

40. Which of the following syntaxes can you use if you want to run three commands so that each command will execute only if the previous exit code is 0?

    A. command1 AND command2 AND command3

    B. command1 || command2 || command3

    C. command1 && command2 && command3

    D. command1 OR command2 OR command3

41. Using bash, you want to list all the **.sh** files in the current working directory. Which of the following commands can you use?

    A. ls -l ???.sh

    B. ls -l *.??

    C. ls -l *.sh

    D. ls -l ?.sh

42. What is the effect of the following command?

    ```
    sed -i 's/a/A/3' file.txt
    ```

    A. It replaces the first three occurrences of the **a** character on each line with the **A** character and overwrites the **file.txt** file

    B. It replaces the first three occurrences of the **a** character on each line with the **A** character and sends the modified text to the standard output

    C. It replaces only the third occurrence of the **a** character on each line with the **A** character and overwrites the **file.txt** file

    D. It replaces only the third occurrence of the **a** character on each line with the **A** character and sends the modified text to the standard output

43. What does the **<<** redirection operator mean?

    A. It causes the contents of the specified file to be used as standard input

    B. It causes the shell to accept text on the following lines as standard input until a specific word is reached. This word has to be on a separate line and without trailing spaces

    C. It expands and passes the string on the right of the operator to the standard input of the command on the left

    D. It is not a redirection operator; if you use it you will get an error message

44. What is the effect of the following command?

```
sed 's/^://' file.txt
```

    A. It removes any colon at the beginning of each line and sends the modified text to the standard output

    B. It removes the first occurrence of ^: on each line and sends the modified text to the standard output

    C. It removes all occurrences of ^: on each line and sends the modified text to the standard output

    D. It deletes any line beginning with colon and sends the modified text to the standard output

45. Your **foobar** task is running in foreground and you want to suspend its execution. Using bash, which of the following keystrokes can you use to achieve this goal?

    A. CTRL+C

    B. CTRL+Z

    C. CTRL+S

    D. CTRL+R

46. Which of the following Systemd targets correspond to the System V **runlevels 0, 1 and 6**?

    A. poweroff.target - emergency.target - reboot.target

    B. reboot.target - single_user_mode.target - poweroff.target

    C. poweroff.target - rescue.target - reboot.target

    D. emergency.target - rescue.target - reboot.target

47. You mount a filesystem over an existing directory (mount point) that already contains files and subdirectories. Which of the following sentences is true?

   A. Files and subdirectories will be lost; you have to recovery them from an existing backup

   B. Files and subdirectories will be no longer visible until the mounted filesystem will be unmounted

   C. Files and subdirectories will be put in the swap space

   D. Files and subdirectories will be lost only if you write on the device

48. Which of the following entries in the **/etc/fstab** file will allow users to mount their CD/DVD?

   A. /dev/sr0   /media/cdrom0   udf,iso9660   nouser,noauto   0   0

   B. /media/cdrom0   /dev/sr0   udf,iso9660   nouser,noauto   0   0

   C. /media/cdrom0   udf,iso9660   user,noauto   0   0

   D. /dev/sr0   /media/cdrom0   udf,iso9660   user,noauto   0   0

49. Which of the following sentences better describes the benefits you can have using containers?

   A. Containers guarantee a fast startup time and a small overhead

   B. Containers are very light (usually only megabytes in size) so that the virtualized hardware can run multiple OS instances

   C. Containers can run a wide variety of different operating systems (Windows, Unix, Linux and so on) on the same physical server

   D. Containers usually add overhead in memory

50. Working with **vi**, you want to move the cursor right ten characters and then down five lines. Which of the following combination keys do you need to press? Assume **vi** is in command mode.

  A. 10l5j

  B. 10l5k

  C. 10h5j

  D. 10h5k

51. What is the effect of the following command?

```
ln dir2 dir1
```

  A. It creates a hard link named **dir1** to the **dir2** directory

  B. It creates a symbolic link **dir1** to the **dir2** directory

  C. It creates a hard link named **dir2** to the **dir1** directory

  D. It creates a symbolic link named **dir2** to the **dir1** directory

  E. It gives you an error message

52. You are performing some actions on the **report.txt** file in your current working directory. Which of the following commands will update the **modify timestamp** on this file? Select two.

  A. echo "EOF" >> report.txt

  B. file report.txt

  C. touch report.txt

  D. cat report.txt

  E. timeupdate report.txt

53. In GRUB 2 you pass the boot parameters from the boot loader to the kernel on the line starting with...

    A. parameters

    B. kernel

    C. options

    D. linux

    E. boot_param

54. According to the FHS, which of the following directories contain static and unshareable files? Select two.

    A. /usr

    B. /opt

    C. /var/mail

    D. /boot

    E. /etc

55. You want to run the **barfoo** command in background so that it will continue running even when you log out of a session or exit the shell (ignoring hangup signals). Which of the following commands can you use to start **barfoo** in order to accomplish this task? Assume you are working with the bash shell.

    A. fg barfoo &

    B. nohangup barfoo &

    C. nohup barfoo &

    D. nosighup barfoo &

    E. sighup barfoo &

56. Working with bash, you want to check if the shell variables named **var_foobar** and **var_barfoo** are defined and, if so, get their value. Which of the following commands can you use to accomplish this task?

   A. set

   B. show

   C. list

   D. env_list

   E. lsenv

57. Which of the following files contains descriptive information about the filesystems the system can mount?

   A. /etc/fstab

   B. /etc/mtab

   C. /etc/filesystems

   D. /etc/mount

   E. /etc/mounts

58. Which of the following statements about **insmod** and **modprobe** is true?

   A. **modprobe** is deprecated and it has been replaced by **insmod**

   B. The two commands are equivalent

   C. **modprobe** is used on Debian derived GNU/Linux systems, while **insmod** on all distributions

   D. **modprobe** is more clever than **insmod** because it can handle module dependencies

59. You want to remove the file named **$file** that you have mistakenly created. Which of the following commands can you use?

    A. rm \$file

    B. rm $file

    C. rm "$file"

    D. rm -- $file

60. Which of the following sentences about MBR disks is true?

    A. MBR disks can hold at most one extended partition

    B. MBR disks can hold at most two extended partitions

    C. MBR disks can hold at most three extended partitions

    D. MBR disks can hold at most four extended partitions

Practice Exam 3

1. You want to extract the first, the third, the fourth and the fifth field of each line from the **/etc/passwd** file. Which of the following commands can you use?

    A. cut -f1,3,4,5 /etc/passwd

    B. cut -f1-5 /etc/passwd

    C. cut -d: -f1-5 /etc/passwd

    D. cut -d: -f1,3-5 /etc/passwd

2. Giving the following:

```
#runlevel

3 5
```

   What can you deduce?

    A. The current runlevel is number 3

    B. The current runlevel is number 5

    C. The system hasn't changed runlevel since booting

    D. The runlevel is in the process of being changed passing from runlevel 3 to runlevel 5

    E. The runlevel is in the process of being changed passing from runlevel 5 to runlevel 3

3. Which of the following syntaxes can you use if you want to run three commands so that the next command will execute only if the previous exit code is not 0?

    A. command1 OR command2 OR command3

    B. command1 || command2 || command3

    C. command1; command2; command3

    D. command1 | command2 | command3

4. Which of the following sentences about your bash history is true?

    A. You can usually find your bash history in the **.bash_history** file in your **home** directory

    B. You can usually find your bash history in the **.hist** file in your **home** directory

    C. You can usually find your bash history in the **.$HISTFILE** file in your **home** directory

    D. You can usually find your bash history in the **.bashist** file in your **home** directory

5. You are examining the GRUB Legacy configuration file and you find **root (hd0,6)**. Which of the following statements is true?

    A. The system is on partition **6** of the first hard drive - **/dev/hda6**

    B. The system is on partition **7** of the first hard drive - **/dev/hda7**

    C. The system is on partition **0** of the sixth hard drive - **/dev/hdf0**

    D. The system is on partition **1** of the sixth hard drive - **/dev/hdf1**

    E. The system is on partition **1** of the seventh hard drive - **/dev/hdg1**

6. You create a hard link **barfoo** to the file named **foobar** and then you accidentally delete the **foobar** file. Which of the following statements is true?

    A. You cannot delete a file if it has hard or symbolic links

    B. **barfoo** will become a broken link

    C. **barfoo** will be deleted

    D. **barfoo** will still exist

7. Assuming your version of **sed** does support extended regular expressions, which of the following options can you use to tell **sed** that you are using the extended syntax?

    A. -r

    B. -e

    C. -i

    D. --extended

    E. --extregexp

8. You want to set recursively the ownership of all files and subdirectories in **/home/barfoo** to **foobar**. Which of the following commands can you use? Select two.

    A. chown -R foobar /home/barfoo

    B. chown -r foobar /home/barfoo

    C. chown --recursive foobar /home/barfoo

    D. chown --rec foobar /home/barfoo

    E. chown -f foobar /home/barfoo

9. The **foo** directory has permissions **drwxr-xr-t**. What is the corresponding octal value?

   A. 2754

   B. 2755

   C. 1754

   D. 1755

10. You want to check the parameters your system was booted up with to verify if the right parameters were passed to the kernel during the boot process. Which file do you need to examine?

    A. /proc/param

    B. /etc/param

    C. /etc/boot/cmdparam

    D. /proc/cmdparam

    E. /proc/cmdline

11. Acting as root, you want to display superblock information including the mount count and the check interval for an **ext3** filesystem. Which of the following commands can you use? Select two.

    A. sblock2fs

    B. dumpe2fs -h

    C. tune2fs -l

    D. e2label

    E. e2superblock -l

12. In the bash shell you execute the **foo 2>1** command. What does the expression **2>1** mean?

    A. It redirects standard error to standard output

    B. It redirects standard error to standard input

    C. It redirects standard output to standard error

    D. It redirects standard error to a file named **1**

13. You want to change the default runlevel of your System V-based system. Which file that consists of lines of four colon-delimited fields do you need to edit? Write the full path.

14. Using bash, what is the effect of the following command? Assume you have the right privileges to execute the script.

```
nice -8 ./script/foobar.sh &
```

    A. The **foobar.sh** script is run in background at a nice level of **8**

    B. The **foobar.sh** script is run in background at a nice level of **-8**

    C. The **foobar.sh** script is run in foreground at a nice level of **8**

    D. The **foobar.sh** script is run in foreground at a nice level of **-8**

15. You want to format a USB key so that the filesystem can be also accessible from Windows. Which of the following commands can you use?

    A. mkfs -t VFAT

    B. mkfs.dos

    C. mkfat

    D. mkfs.vfat

16. Giving the following:

```
$jobs

[1]    Stopped   xeyes

[2] -  Stopped   xcalc

[3]    Stopped   ./script/script.sh

[4] +  Stopped   xclock
```

What happens if you type the **bg** command in the bash shell?

    A. The **xeyes** application will be started in background

    B. The **xcalc** application will be started in background

    C. The **script.sh** script will be started in background

    D. The **xclock** application will be started in background

17. Which of the following sentences about an **IaaS** architecture is true?

    A. It is a cloud model in which a provider hosts and manages the entire infrastructure and delivers software and applications for users

    B. It is a cloud model in which a provider hosts the infrastructure components (servers, storage, networking hardware) and provides an environment in which users can develop, manage and deliver their applications

    C. It is a cloud model in which a provider hosts the infrastructure components (servers, storage, networking hardware) and the hypervisor layer and also provides a range of useful services such as log access, monitoring, backup, security and so on

    D. It is a model in which a company has its own on-site servers and requires the help of a consulting society to install, maintain and upgrade its entire in-house server infrastructure

18. You want to verify all packages on your RPM-based distribution by comparing the information of the installed files in each package with those of the files taken from the package metadata stored in the rpm database. Which of the following commands can you use?

    A. rpm -qa

    B. rpm -Va

    C. rpm -va

    D. rpm -v

19. According to the FHS, which of the following directories can be considered for a separate partition if it will probably contain a lot of variable data files such as spool directories and files, administrative and logging data and transient and temporary files?

    A. /lib

    B. /usr

    C. /var

    D. /etc

20. In the bash shell you type the **xclock** command forgetting the **&** character to launch it in background. What can you do to bring it from foreground to background?

    A. First suspend the job with **CTRL+C** and then type the **bg** command

    B. Close the bash shell and type the **bg** command in a new shell

    C. First suspend the job with **CTRL+Z** and then type the **bg** command

    D. Close the bash shell and type the **bg xclock** command in a new shell

21. You want to find which package contains a specified file (for example **foobar**) on a Debian derived GNU/Linux system. Which action of the **dpkg** command can you use?

    A. -P

    B. -L

    C. -i

    D. -S

22. Working with the **vi** editor, you want to move the cursor at the end of the current line. Which of the following keys do you need to press? Assume **vi** is in command mode.

    A. 0

    B. $

    C. o

    D. O

23. What is the effect of the following command?

```
date | tee -a date_time
```

    A. The result of the **date** command is sent to the standard error and to the **date_time** command

    B. The result of the **date** command is sent to the standard output and appended to the file named **date_time**

    C. The result of the **date** command is sent to the **tee** and **date_time** commands

    D. The result of the **date** command is appended to the **tee** and **date_time** files

24. You want to adjust the number of mounts after which the filesystem will be checked by **e2fsck**, setting the maximum mount count to 20. Which option of the **tune2fs** command can you use?

    A. -C

    B. -c

    C. -E

    D. -e

    E. --ext-mounts

25. Type codes of MBR partitions are 1-byte (two-digit hexadecimal) numbers. What is the type code (ID Number) of a Linux data partition?

    A. 0x05

    B. 0x0f

    C. 0x82

    D. 0x83

26. You want to change the number of commands that will be saved in your history file. Which variable do you need to edit? Assume you are working with the bash shell.

    A. HIST_SIZE

    B. HISTSIZE

    C. HIST_NUMBER

    D. SIZE_HIST

    E. SIZEHIST

27. You want to have information about the interrupts on the system and about DMA channels in use. Which of the following files within the **/proc** tree can you examine to accomplish this task?

    A. /proc/tuneirq and /proc/dmachannels

    B. /proc/interrupts and /proc/dma

    C. /proc/irqs and /proc/channels

    D. /proc/interrupt and /proc/dma_channels

28. **/dev/hdd1** represents...

    A. the first primary partition of the secondary master on the secondary IDE controller

    B. the first primary partition of the primary master on the primary IDE controller

    C. the first primary partition of the secondary slave on the secondary IDE controller

    D. the first primary partition of the primary slave on the primary IDE controller

29. You want to decompress the **part1 part2 part3.bz2** file (with 2 spaces in the file name). Which of the following commands can you use? Select two.

    A. bunzip2 \part1 part2 part3.bz2

    B. bunzip2 part1\ part2\ part3.bz2

    C. bzip2 -d part1' 'part2' 'part3.bz2

    D. bunzip2 part1 part2 part3.bz2

    E. bzip2 -d 'part1' 'part2' 'part3'.bz2

30. You have installed another OS (with its own bootloader) on your machine and now you need to reinstall GRUB Legacy to the **/dev/sdb** device. Which of the following commands can you use? Assume you are acting as root.

    A. install-grub /dev/sdb

    B. grub-install /dev/sdb

    C. mkgrub /dev/sdb

    D. mkconfig /dev/sdb

31. Which of the following statements about basic and extended regular expressions is true?

    A. In basic regular expressions some meta-characters such as **?**, **+** or ***** lose the special meaning they have in extended regular expressions; if you want to use the functions of these characters in basic regular expressions you have to escape them with a backslash

    B. In extended regular expressions some meta-characters such as **?**, **+** or ***** lose the special meaning they have in basic regular expressions; if you want to use the functions of these characters in extended regular expressions you have to escape them with a backslash

    C. In basic regular expressions some special meta-characters such as **?**, **+** or ***** have to be escaped with a backslash in order to be treated as literal characters

    D. In extended regular expressions some meta-characters such as **?**, **+** or ***** have a special meaning, but there is no way to treat them as literal characters. In such cases you have to use basic regular expressions in which these meta-characters lose their special meaning

32. You want to display useful hardware information about USB buses in your Linux system and the devices connected to them (for example the keyboard, the external disk drive or the printer). Which command can you use to accomplish this task? Write only the command name.

33. You are attempting to unmount a filesystem, but you get an error message. Which of the following commands can you use to check if the filesystem you want to unmount has open files?

    A. listf

    B. file

    C. lsfile

    D. lsof

34. Acting as root, you have written a command line application named **foobar** on your local system and now you want to distribute it to all users. According to the FHS, where do you need to put your custom executable file so that it can be used by the other users in the system? Assume **foobar** has the required permissions correctly set.

    A. /usr/sbin

    B. /usr/share

    C. /usr/local/bin

    D. /usr/programs/common/share

35. In the bash shell the **foo** user types:

```
echo 'I am $USER'
```

What will be the result?

    A. I am foo

    B. I am USER

    C. I am $USER

    D. An error message will be displayed

36. You want to show the list of every process in the system, also showing the processes not attached to a terminal. Which of the following commands can you use? Assume your version of **ps** accepts UNIX options, BSD options and GNU long options.

    A. ps au

    B. ps -a

    C. ps aux

    D. ps -l

37. Which of the following options can you specify in the **/etc/fstab** file in order to allow a regular user to mount a particular filesystem? Select two.

    A. owners

    B. user

    C. allow_users

    D. users

    E. nouser

38. You want to find out the PIDs of the running tasks in your current shell so that you can suspend those that are using more resources. Which of the following commands can you use? Select two.

    A. lsproc

    B. job

    C. ps

    D. jobs

    E. free

39. Working with **vi**, you want to search backward for occurrences of the **home** string inside the text. Which of the following commands can you use? Assume **vi** is in command mode.

    A. ?home

    B. /home

    C. /?home

    D. ?/home

40. You want to upgrade the **pkgfoobar.rpm** package only if an earlier version already exists. Which of the following commands can you use? Assume you are working with a RPM-based distribution.

    A. rpm -Uvh pkgfoobar.rpm

    B. rpm -ivh pkgfoobar.rpm

    C. rpm -Fvh pkgfoobar.rpm

    D. rpm --upgrade -hv pkgfoobar.rpm

41. According to the new EFI principles, which of the following statements about EFI boot loaders is true?

    A. Boot loaders are stored in various boot sectors such as the boot sector of a disk partition or the Master Boot Record of a hard drive

    B. There can only be one boot loader inside a EFI System Partition (ESP)

    C. The EFI System Partition (ESP) in which boot loaders can be found uses the ext4 or XFS filesystems

    D. Boot loaders reside in .efi files stored in a partition on the hard disk known as EFI System Partition (ESP)

42. You have just created a new file named **foo** inside your system, but when you use the **locate** command to search for it, it gives no results. How can you solve this situation? Assume you are acting as root.

    A. You have to use the **apt-get update** command to update your system

    B. You have to use the **updatedb** command to update the **locate** database

    C. You have to restart your system

    D. You have to use the **dbupdate** command to update the **locate** database

43. What's the meaning of the following command?

```
cp $(find . -type f -name '*.sh') /tmp
```

    A. It copies all the regular **.sh** files in the current directory to **/tmp**

    B. It copies all the regular files in the current directory to **/tmp**

    C. It copies all the regular files in the current directory and in all subdirectories to **/tmp**

    D. It copies all the regular **.sh** files in the current directory and in all subdirectories to **/tmp**

44. Which of the following operators can you use in bash redirections? Select two.

    A. &>

    B. ||

    C. >>

    D. &

    E. &&

45. The **bar** user creates a program named **foo**. What is the minimum nice value that this ordinary user can set for **foo** when he uses the **nice** command?

    A. -20

    B. -19

    C. 19

    D. 20

    E. 0

46. You want to remove the **pkgfoobar** package on a Debian derived GNU/Linux system, along with packages that were installed as dependencies but no longer required by any installed packages. Which command can you use?

    A. apt-get autoremove pkgfoobar

    B. apt-cache autoremove pkgfoobar

    C. apt-cache remove pkgfoobar

    D. apt-get remove pkgfoobar

    E. apt-cache delete pkgfoobar

47. Which of the following statements about hard links are true? Select two.

    A. Hard links cannot span across different filesystems

    B. Hard links point to the same inode

    C. Hard links can be used for directories

    D. When you remove the original file the hard link will become a broken link

    E. When you remove the original file the hard link will be deleted

48. Using the Bash shell, you want to set **vi** as your default text editor. Which of the following commands can you use?

    A. export vi=EDITOR

    B. set -o vi=EDITOR

    C. set -o EDITOR=vi

    D. export EDITOR=vi

49. What is the effect of the following command? Assume the **foo** file consists of 110 lines.

```
split -l25 foo
```

    A. The **foo** file will be split into 25 output files based on its size, each of which will have a name that consists of a prefix **y** followed by a group of letters: **aa**, **ab**, **ac** and so on.

    B. The **foo** file will be split into 25 output files based on its size, each of which will have a name that consists of a prefix **x** followed by a group of letters: **aa**, **ab**, **ac** and so on.

    C. The **foo** file will be split into 5 files: **yaa** of 25 lines, **yab** of 25 lines, **yac** of 25 lines, **yad** of 25 lines and **yae** of 10 lines.

    D. The **foo** file will be split into 5 files: **xaa** of 25 lines, **xab** of 25 lines, **xac** of 25 lines, **xad** of 25 lines and **xae** of 10 lines.

50. What's the meaning of the | meta-character in regular expressions?

    A. It represents any single character except newlines

    B. It separates two possible matches

    C. It indicates boundary of a word

    D. The literal | character

51. Which of the following boot parameters can you pass to the kernel from the boot loader to boot Systemd in single user mode to perform rescue operations? Assume you are using Systemd as system and service manager.

    A. systemd.default_runlevel=runlevel1.target

    B. systemd.target=emergency.target

    C. systemd.unit=rescue.target

    D. systemd.target=single-user-mode.target

52. Using **yum** or **zypper,** which of the following subcommands can you use to search for packages matching any of the given search strings (for example the **gcc** keyword)?

    A. locate

    B. search

    C. query

    D. mlocate

    E. find

53. What is the effect of the following command?

    ```
    foobar | barfoo
    ```

    A. The **stdout** of **foobar** is appended to the **barfoo** file

    B. The **stdout** of **barfoo** is forwarded to the **stdin** of **foobar**

    C. The **stdout** of **foobar** is forwarded to the **stdin** of **barfoo**

    D. The **stdout** of **barfoo** is appended to the **foobar** file

    E. The **stdout** and **stderr** of **foobar** is appended to the **barfoo** file

54. You want to reconfigure the already installed **foo** package on a Debian derived GNU/Linux system. Which of the following commands can you use?

    A. reconfiguredpkg foo

    B. dpkg-reconfigure foo

    C. apt-get reconfigure foo

    D. apt-cache reconfigure foo

    E. dpkgreconfigure foo

55. You want to print the shared libraries required by your custom executable named **foobar**. Which of the following utilities can you use?

    A. ld

    B. ldd

    C. ldcache

    D. ldconfig

    E. lddconfig

56. You want to mount your CD-ROM to **/media/cdrom0**. Which of the following commands can you use? Assume you have already mounted the filesystem and you have already a correct entry in the **/etc/fstab** file.

    A. auto-mount -t cdrom /media/cdrom0

    B. mount /mnt/cdrom0

    C. mount /media/cdrom0

    D. mount -t cdrom /media/cdrom0

57. You want to burn an **iso image** to a USB drive. Which of the following utilities can you use?

    A. mkiso

    B. cc

    C. dd

    D. mkiso2usb

    E. usb2iso

58. Which file name represents the default target unit used when the Linux system boots? Assume your system uses Systemd as system and service manager.

    A. default.target

    B. default.runlevel

    C. target.default

    D. runlevel.default

59. The **foo** directory has the sticky bit set. What is its meaning?

    A. The files in the **foo** directory can be deleted only by their owners

    B. The files in the **foo** directory can be deleted only by their owners, the directory' s owner and root

    C. The files in the **foo** directory can be deleted only by root

    D. The files in the **foo** directory can be created and deleted by everyone

    E. All executable files in the **foo** directory are run with the permissions of the file owner rather than the user who runs it

60. You want to extract files from the compressed archive named **archive.tar.gz**.
    Which of the following commands can you use?

   A. tar -tvf archive.tar.gz

   B. tar --gzip-extract --file-name archive.tar.gz

   C. tar -xzvf archive.tar.gz

   D. zcat archive.tar.gz

Practice Exam 4

1. You want to print system information such as the kernel name, the kernel release, the processor type and the operating system. Which of the following commands can you use?

    A. system

    B. show

    C. uname

    D. lsinfo

    E. cname

2. Using bash, what is the effect of the following command?

    ```
    cat view.txt view1.txt view2.txt view3.txt &> output.txt
    ```

    Assume not all the specified files exist in the current working directory.

    A. The contents of all valid files are redirected to **output.txt**

    B. The errors generated by invalid files are redirected to **output.txt**

    C. Both the contents of all valid files and the errors generated by invalid files are redirected to **output.txt**

    D. The contents of all valid files are printed on the terminal, while the errors generated by invalid files are redirected to **output.txt**

3. You want to look at the **nice** value of the processes running in your bash terminal to find out which one has higher scheduling priority. Which of the following commands can you use? Select two.

   A. nice

   B. jobs

   C. ps

   D. top

   E. lsproc

4. Your **foobar** command is running in foreground, but you press **CTRL+C** on the keyboard to interrupt its execution. What signal is sent to **foobar** and what is its numerical value?

   A. SIGKILL (9)

   B. SIGSTOP (19)

   C. SIGTSTP (20)

   D. SIGINT (2)

5. What's the meaning of the following permissions?

   ```
   -rwsr-xr-x 1 root root 51096 feb 10 2015 foo
   ```

   A. The sticky bit is set - The **foo** command runs with root privileges

   B. The SUID bit is set - The **foo** command runs with root privileges

   C. The SGID bit is set - The **foo** command runs with root privileges

   D. Only root can run the **foo** command

   E. Only root and members of the **sudo** group can run the **foo** command

6. You want to remove the **pkgfoobar** package, including configuration files, on a Debian derived GNU/Linux system. Which of the following commands can you use?

   A. dpkg -P pkgfoobar

   B. dpkg -p pkgfoobar

   C. dpkg -r pkgfoobar

   D. dpkg -C pkgfoobar

7. You want to locate the binary, source and manual page files for the **foobar** command. Which of the following utilities can you use?

   A. which

   B. whereis

   C. locate

   D. search

8. You are performing a search using the **vi** editor (for example of the **home** string in your text). Which key can you press to move to the next occurrence of your search string?

   A. t

   B. z

   C. m

   D. n

9. You mounted a USB drive on your system, but you don't remember its mount point and its mount options. Which file under **/etc** can you examine to list all currently mounted filesystems so that you can retrieve the information you need? Write the full path.

10. The **telinit** command takes a one-character argument and signals **init** to perform the appropriate action. Which of the following arguments can you pass to this command to tell **init** to re-examine the **/etc/inittab** file? Select two.

    A. Q

    B. q

    C. s

    D. U

    E. u

11. You are examining a live log file. Which option of the **tail** command can be useful to monitor log files for updates in such cases?

    A. -n

    B. -c

    C. -f

    D. -v

12. You want to change the name of the file where the command history is saved. Which variable do you need to edit? Assume you are working with the bash shell.

    A. HIST_FILE_NAME

    B. HISTORY_FILE_NAME

    C. HISTORY_FILE

    D. HISTFILE

    E. HIST_FILE

13. Using System V, which of the following boot parameters can you pass to the kernel from the boot loader to boot in single user mode to perform rescue operations? Select two.

    A. debug

    B. single

    C. s

    D. single-mode

    E. single-user

14. You start the **foo** program using the **nice** command without specifying any adjustment value. So **foo** is started at a nice value of...

    A. 0

    B. -20

    C. 10

    D. -19

    E. 20

15. Working as root, you want to print the name, the UUID, the filesystem type and the volume label of the device named **/dev/sda1**. Which of the following commands can you use? Select two.

    A. blkid /dev/sda1

    B. lsblock /dev/sda1

    C. lsblk -o NAME,UUID,FSTYPE,LABEL /dev/sda1

    D. blkid -o NAME,UUID,FSTYPE,LABEL /dev/sda1

    E. lsblockdev -o NAME,UUID,FSTYPE,LABEL /dev/sda1

16. You want to know what I/O addresses the computer is using for communicating with devices. Which file within the **/proc** tree can you examine to accomplish this task? Write the full path.

17. What's the meaning of the following command?

```
grep -E '[aeiou]{2,}' report.txt
```

    A. It finds any line in the **report.txt** file with one or two vowels

    B. It finds any line in the **report.txt** file with two or more vowels in a row

    C. It finds any line in the **report.txt** file with two or more vowels

    D. It finds any line in the **report.txt** file with only two vowels

18. Which of the following statements about the **renice** command is true?

    A. It is deprecated and it has been replaced by the **nice** command

    B. An ordinary user can use it to give his processes higher or lower scheduling priority and make them less or more nice

    C. An ordinary user must run the command as superuser if he wants to give his processes higher scheduling priority and make them less nice

    D. An ordinary user can use the **renice** command to launch a program with an adjusted niceness, but he can only specify positive adjustment values

19. You want to install a GRUB Legacy image under a custom directory instead of the root directory. Which long option of the **grub-install** command can you use?

    A. --custom-dir

    B. --custom

    C. --root

    D. --root-directory

20. The **defaults** option that you can specify in the **/etc/fstab** file includes... Select two.

    A. the rw option

    B. the ro option

    C. the user option

    D. the users option

    E. the auto option

21. Using GRUB Legacy, you pass the boot parameters from the boot loader to the kernel on the...

    A. kernel line

    B. options line

    C. boot line

    D. linux line

22. Which of the following statements about **initial ram disk** is true?

    A. It is mainly designed to speed up the system boot without providing any support to the kernel for the root filesystem mounting

    B. It is mainly designed to be used when the amount of physical memory (RAM) is full

    C. It is mainly designed to allow system startup to occur in two phases, where the kernel comes up with a minimum set of compiled-in drivers and where additional modules are loaded from initrd

    D. It is mainly designed to allow a boot loader to boot a second boot loader (chain loading)

23. You want to reboot your system in one hour, sending the warning message "Restart needed for maintenance: kernel upgrade" to all connected users. Which of the following commands can you use?

    A. shutdown -r +1 Restart needed for maintenance: kernel upgrade

    B. shutdown -r +60 Restart needed for maintenance: kernel upgrade

    C. shutdown -r +1 -m Restart needed for maintenance: kernel upgrade

    D. shutdown -r +60 --messages Restart needed for maintenance: kernel upgrade

24. You prefer the **vi** editor to **Emacs**; so you can use a **vi-like mode** in bash by typing...

    A. set -o vi=EDITOR

    B. set -o EDITOR=vi

    C. set -o vi

    D. set --disable emacs; set --enable vi

    E. set --disable vi; set --enable emacs

25. On a Debian derived GNU/Linux system you want to clear out the local repository of retrieved package files removing only package files that can no longer be downloaded. Which of the following commands can you use?

    A. apt-get clean

    B. apt-get autoclean

    C. apt-cache autoclean

    D. apt-cache clean

26. You want to search for a pattern in a file using extended regular expressions. Which of the following commands can you use? Select two.

    A. rgrep

    B. grep

    C. grep -E

    D. egrep

    E. grep -F

27. You want to remove the **foo** directory and its contents recursively. Which of the following commands can you use? Assume **foo** is in your current working directory.

    A. rm -r foo

    B. rm foo

    C. rm -r foo/*

    D. rmdir -r foo

    E. rmdir foo

28. You want to disable the **RPMrepo** repository that you have previously added. Which of the following commands can you use? Assume you are using **Zypper** as command line tool for package management in your OpenSUSE or SUSE Enterprise Linux platform.

    A. zypper removerepo RPMrepo

    B. zypper modifyrepo -d RPMrepo

    C. zypper disablerepo RPMrepo

    D. zypper removerepo --disable RPMrepo

29. What's the meaning of the following command?

```
ls -l /foobar/[a-z][a-z][a-z]1
```

    A. It lists all four-character files in the **/foobar** directory

    B. It lists all four-character files beginning by three lowercase characters followed by the digit 1 in the **/foobar** directory

    C. It lists all files beginning by a lowercase character or by the digit 1 in the **/foobar** directory

    D. It lists all files beginning by three lowercase characters in the **/foobar** directory

30. Type codes of MBR partitions are 1-byte (two-digit hexadecimal) numbers. What is the type code (ID Number) of a Linux swap partition?

    A. 0x82

    B. 0x83

    C. 0x05

    D. 0x0f

31. Which of the following statements about **locate** and **find** are true? Select two.

    A. **locate** can perform more complex searches than **find** (for example by name, type, size and so on)

    B. **locate** may not find recent files or it may return the names of files that no longer exist

    C. **find** is deprecated and it has been replaced by **locate**

    D. **locate** is deprecated and it has been replaced by **find**

    E. **locate** is usually much faster than find

32. In the bash shell you execute a series of commands and scripts in background and then you type the **jobs** command. What is the result?

    A. You obtain a dynamic real-time view of the running system (a list of processes currently being managed by the Linux kernel and system summary information)

    B. You obtain the list of jobs associated with all terminals and their job numbers

    C. You obtain the list of jobs associated with your terminal and the list of jobs associated with the parent shell

    D. You obtain the list of jobs associated with your terminal and their job numbers

33. Acting with root privileges, you want to display the partition tables for the GPT-formatted disk named **/dev/sdc**. Which of the following commands can you use?

    A. gdisk -l /dev/sdc

    B. gptable -l /dev/sdc

    C. cat /etc/fstab

    D. gptdisk /dev/sdc

34. You want to create a symbolic link named **foo** to the **bar** file. Which of the following commands can you use? Select two.

    A. link -s bar foo

    B. ln -s bar foo

    C. cp -l bar foo

    D. cp -s bar foo

    E. ln bar foo

35. You have mistakenly created the **\report.txt** file inside the **home** directory of the **foobar** user and you want to rename it in **report.txt**. Which of the following commands can you use? Assume you are acting as root.

    A. mv "~foobar/\report.txt" ~foobar/report.txt

    B. mv ~foobar/\\report.txt ~foobar/report.txt

    C. mv ~foobar/\report.txt ~foobar/report.txt

    D. mv '~foobar\\report.txt' ~foobar/report.txt

36. What is the effect of the following command?

```
foobar < foo
```

    A. The **foo** command puts its output into the **foobar** file

    B. The **foobar** command puts its output into the **foo** file

    C. The **foobar** command gets its input from the **foo** file

    D. The **foo** command gets its input from the **foobar** file

37. You want to have the default permissions rw-rw-r-- for new files and rwxrwxr-x for new directories. How should you set the umask value? Write only the numerical umask value without the digit that represents the octal code for SUID, SGID and the sticky bit.

38. The sticky bit is a special permission that is useful in world-writable directories. In which of the following directories is this permission usually set?

    A. /usr

    B. /root

    C. /tmp

    D. None of the above

39. Acting with root privileges, you want to convert the **ext2** filesystem on **/dev/sda2** to an **ext3** filesystem by adding the journal. Which of the following commands can you use?

    A. dumpe2fs -E /dev/sda2

    B. conv2ext3 -j /dev/sda2

    C. e2fsck -E /dev/sda2

    D. tune2fs -j /dev/sda2

40. You want to extract files from the compressed archive named **archive.tar.bz2**. Which of the following commands can you use?

    A. bzcat archive.tar.bz2

    B. tar -tvf archive.tar.bz2

    C. tar -xzvf archive.tar.bz2

    D. bzcat archive.tar.bz2 | tar -xvf -

    E. zcat archive.tar.bz2 | tar -xvf -

41. The **foobar** user wants to test an experimental version of the **test.so** library in the **lib** directory inside his **home**. What can he do?

    A. He adds the **/home/foobar/lib** directory to the **/etc/ld.so.conf** file and then he runs **ldconfig**

    B. He adds the **/home/foobar/lib** directory to the **/etc/ld.so.cache** file and then he runs **ldconfig**

    C. He adds the **/home/foobar/lib** directory to the **LD_LIBRARY_PATH** variable and then he exports the variable

    D. He runs the **ldd /home/foobar/lib** command and then he reboots the system

42. You want to show a summary of the disk space used on all of a system's partitions, displaying also their mount points. Which of the following utilities can you use?

    A. du

    B. df

    C. free

    D. lsusage

43. What is the effect of the following command?

```
foobar | barfoo > bar
```

    A. The **foobar** command sends its output to the **barfoo** file and its errors to the **bar** file

    B. The **barfoo** command gets its input from the **foobar** command and sends its output to the **bar** file

    C. The **foobar** command gets its input from the **barfoo** command and sends its output to the **bar** file

    D. The **bar** command gets its input from the **barfoo** command and sends its output to the **foobar** file

    E. The **foobar** command sends its output to the **bar** file and its errors to the **barfoo** file

44. **/dev/sda5** represents...

    A. the fifth primary partition on the first SCSI disk

    B. the first logical partition on the first SCSI disk

    C. the fifth extended partition on the first SCSI disk

    D. the first extended partition on the first SCSI disk

45. Using the **yum** package manager, you want to find out which RPM package provides the **ft_barfoo** feature so that you can install it on your system through the **yum install** command. Which of the following commands can you use?

    A. yum whatprovides ft_barfoo

    B. yum info ft_barfoo

    C. yum deplist ft_barfoo

    D. yum check-feature ft_barfoo

46. You want to delete all files belonging to the user with **uid** 1001. Which of the following commands can you use?

    A. xargs rm (find / -type f -user 1001)

    B. find / -type f -user 1001 | rm xargs

    C. find / -type f -user 1001 | rm -f

    D. find / -type f -user 1001 | xargs rm -f

47. Using Systemd as system and service manager, you want to configure the **srv_barfoo** service to start when the computer boots next (auto-start at system boot). Which of the following commands can you use?

    A. systemctl insert srv_barfoo.service

    B. systemctl start srv_barfoo.service

    C. systemctl enable srv_barfoo.service

    D. systemctl activate srv_barfoo.service

48. You want to display useful hardware information about PCI buses in your Linux system and the devices connected to them (for example the Ethernet card or the video card). Which command can you use to accomplish this task? Write only the command name.

49. What is the name of the main configuration file for GRUB Legacy normally and which one for GRUB 2?

    A. **/boot/grub/grub.cfg** for GRUB Legacy and **/boot/grub/grub.conf** or **/boot/grub/menu.lst** for GRUB 2

    B. **/boot/grub/grub.conf** or **/boot/grub/menu.lst** for GRUB Legacy and **/boot/grub/grub.cfg** for GRUB 2

    C. **/boot/grub/grub.cfg** for GRUB Legacy and **/boot/grub/grub2.cfg** for GRUB 2

    D. **/boot/grub/grub.cfg** for both GRUB Legacy and GRUB 2

50. Working with **vi**, you want to delete the entire current line and the next 10 lines. Which sequence of keys will accomplish this task? Assume **vi** is in insert mode.

    A. ESC 11yy

    B. ESC 11dd

    C. 11xx

    D. 11dd

    E. ESC 11xx

51. You want to print a list of all your current environment variables to see which ones are set. Which of the following commands can you use?

    A. set-env

    B. show

    C. print-env

    D. env

    E. list-variables

52. You are planning to create a file server that will hold a lot of users' data. According to the FHS, which of the following directories can you consider for a separate partition in order to preserve users' data files during a system upgrade or in case you have to reinstall the file server?

    A. /lib

    B. /home

    C. /tmp

    D. /usr

53. You want to install the newest available versions of all packages currently installed on your system, based on locally stored information about available packages. Which of the following commands can you use? Assume you are working on a Debian derived GNU/Linux system.

    A. apt-get upgrade

    B. apt-get update

    C. apt-cache upgrade

    D. apt-cache update

    E. apt-get distribution-upgrade

54. You want to search for all occurrences of your DNS servers **192.168.1.10** and **192.168.1.11** in all files under **/etc**. Which of the following commands can you use?

    A. grep -r -E '\(192.168.1.10\|192.168.1.11\)' /etc/

    B. grep -r '(192.168.1.10|192.168.1.11)' /etc/

    C. grep -r -E '\(192.168.1.10|192.168.1.11\)' /etc/

    D. grep -r '\(192.168.1.10\|192.168.1.11\)' /etc/

55. Which of the following statements about symbolic links is true?

    A. Symbolic links can span across different filesystems

    B. Symbolic links are directory entries that point to the same inode

    C. Symbolic links cannot be used for directories

    D. When you remove the original file the symbolic link will be deleted

56. In **IaaS** clouds it is often useful to clone an existing virtual machine. Which of the following statements is true?

    A. The original virtual machine can be cloned only if it has been previously converted in a template

    B. The new virtual machine can be powered on and deployed in the environment without any changes

    C. The new virtual machine can be powered on and deployed in the environment paying attention that new changes to the original virtual machine will be reflected in the cloned virtual machine and new changes to the cloned virtual machine will be reflected in the original virtual machine

    D. The new virtual machine can be powered on and deployed in the environment after changing its unique system information (system name and network settings) to prevent any network conflicts

57. Using the **vi** editor in command mode, you type **:!ls**. What is the result?

    A. The **ls** string is searched within the text

    B. The external command **ls** is executed

    C. The **l** character is replaced by the **s** character within the text

    D. The **s** character is replaced by the **l** character within the text

58. You want to print line numbers only before each non empty line in the **report.txt** file. Which of the following commands can you use? Select two.

    A. cat -n report.txt

    B. nl -bt report.txt

    C. cat -b report.txt

    D. cat report.txt

    E. nl -ba report.txt

59. Which of the following commands can you use to look up processes and send them a specified signal, using selection criteria based on name and other attributes?

    A. watch - pkill

    B. jobs - killall

    C. jobs - kill

    D. pgrep - pkill

60. You want to extract data from the **pkgfoobar.rpm** package without installing it. Which of the following commands can you use?

    A. rpm --extract pkgfoobar.rpm > foobar

    B. rpm --extract-archive2tar pkgfoobar.rpm | tar -xvf

    C. extract-rpm --cpio pkgfoobar.rpm | cpio -idmv

    D. rpm2cpio pkgfoobar.rpm | cpio -i --make-directories

Answers

Answers to the Practice Exam 1

1. **B, E - Topic 103.1**

   The **pwd** command is used to print the full filename of the current working directory, making option B the correct answer. In order to accomplish the same task, you can also display the value of the **PWD** environment variable as stated in option E. The **cat** command is used to concatenate files, or standard input, to standard output, while the **WD** environment variable does not exist by default. Therefore, options C and D are incorrect. Finally, option A prints the **WORKING_DIR** string to standard output and so this option is incorrect.

2. **C - Topic 103.8**

   Typing **i** the **vi** editor will insert text before the cursor, while typing **a** it will append text after the cursor. Typing **I** the **vi** editor will insert text at the beginning of the current line, while typing **A** it will append text at the end of the current line. Therefore, option C is the correct answer.

3. **C - Topic 104.5**

   The **chown** command is used to change file owner and group and therefore option C is the correct answer. The question specifies you have root privileges and so you can always perform this operation, contrary to what is stated in option A. For completeness, the **chmod** command (option B) is used to change file permissions, while the **chgrp** (option D) command is used to change group ownership.

4. D - Topic 103.4

The command shows an example of redirection. In this case, the standard error is redirected to the current location of the standard output and then the standard output is redirected to the **report.txt** file. This second redirection does not affect the standard error, but only the standard output. So an error message is printed on the terminal (because the **view.txt** file does not exist) and an empty file named **report.txt** is created. This makes option D the correct answer.

5. A - Topic 104.7

The **which** command searches for your path for the command you type and lists the full pathname to the first match it finds. Therefore, option A is the correct answer. The **locate** command is used to find a file by name and so option B is incorrect. The **lookup** and **search** commands are not valid and this makes options C and D the incorrect answers.

6. D - Topic 101.2

The kernel keeps its output messages into the so called kernel ring buffer. In order to print these messages to the standard output, you can use the **dmesg** command. Therefore, option D is the correct answer. In **/var/log/messages** you can find a lot of useful log information (that can be filtered through the **grep** utility), but not the messages of the kernel ring buffer; so options A and B are incorrect. The **kmesg** command is not valid and this makes option C the incorrect answer.

7. C - Topic 102.4

On Debian-based systems **apt-cache** performs a variety of operations on APT's package cache. You can use the **search** subcommand to perform a full text search on all available package lists for the specified pattern. This makes option C the correct answer. Options A, B and D contain invalid subcommands and are therefore incorrect.

8. unset - Topic 103.1

The **unset** command is used to remove both environment and user-defined variables.

9. B - Topic 103.2

The **sort** command is used to sort the contents of a text file, line by line, and so it is the right command to use. The question specifies to use the Surname field as sort field and so you have to indicate it using the -k option of this command. The question also specifies to delete duplicate lines; therefore, you can pipe the results of the **sort** command to **uniq**, making option B the correct answer. For completeness, the **uniq** command is used to report or filter out repeated lines in a file and the -d option of this command is used to print only duplicate lines.

10. A - Topic 103.1

The **echo** command is used to print the value of an environment variable to the standard output and therefore option A is the correct answer. The **cat** command is used to concatenate files, or standard input, to standard output and this makes option B incorrect. Option C prints the **SHELL** string to standard output, while option D refers to the **vi** editor (visual editor) and so these options are incorrect.

11. D - Topic 103.3

The **rm** command is used to remove files or directories. In order to remove a file, whose name begins with a dash, you can specify a double dash separately before the file name so that the **rm** command does not misinterpret the file name as an option. For this reason, option D is the correct answer.

12. tee - Topic 103.4

The **tee** command reads from standard input and sends its output both to standard output and to one or more files. It is primarily used in conjunction with pipes and filters.

13. D - Topic 102.3

The **LD_LIBRARY_PATH** environment variable specifies additional directories where library files may be found. This makes option D the correct answer.

14. C, D - Topic 102.1

The **/boot** and **/home** directories are commonly split off into separate partitions. In particular, the **/home** directory holds user data files, while the **/boot** directory holds boot files. The **/bin**, **/sbin** and **/lib** directories contain essential command binaries, essential system binaries, and essential shared libraries and kernel modules, respectively, and should never be placed on separate partitions. This makes options C and D the correct answers.

15. B - Topic 104.6

A symbolic link is a special file that points to a directory or to another file by name. When you delete the original file the symbolic link will become a broken link. Therefore, option B is the correct answer, while options C and D are incorrect. Option A contains a wrong statement and is therefore incorrect.

16. B - Topic 103.4

Option B describes the effect of the command correctly: in fact, **barfoo** is started with the output of **foobar** as arguments. For completeness, option A reverses the order of **barfoo** and **foobar**, while options C and D contain a wrong description of the effect of the command (**xargs** does not start **foobar** and **barfoo** and is not a file, but a command that builds and executes command lines from standard input).

17. /etc/apt/sources.list - Topic 102.4

The package resource list on Debian-based systems is located in **/etc/apt/sources.list.** In addition, any file ending with **.list** in **/etc/apt/sources.list.d** is included.

18.C - Topic 102.5

On a RPM-based distribution, **rpm** is a Package Manager, which can be used to install, build, query, update, erase and manage packages. You can use the -f (--file) option of the **rpm** command with the -q operation to know the package that owns a specified file. Therefore, option C is the correct answer. For completeness, the -l option with the -q operation (option A) is used to display the files contained in the specified package, the -U option (option B) is used to install a new package or to upgrade an existing one, the -i option with the -q operation (option D) is used to display package information and the -F option (option E) is used to upgrade packages, but only ones for which an earlier version is installed.

19.C - Topic 104.2

The **du** command is used to summarize disk usage of each file given as parameter, recursively for directories. So you can use this command if you want to know the total space used by the **/home** directory and all its subdirectories. The **du** command has not a -r option and therefore option C is the correct answer, while option D is incorrect. The **df** command is used to report file system disk space usage and so options A and B are incorrect.

20.D - Topic 103.1

If you want to run more commands in sequence, regardless of whether the previous ones failed or not, you can separate them with semicolons. If you want to execute more commands so that each command will execute only if the previous one succeeded (exit code 0), you can combine them using the **&&** operator. Otherwise, if you want to execute more commands so that each command will execute only if the previous one failed (exit code not 0), you can combine them using the **||** operator. Therefore, option D is the correct answer, while options A and B are incorrect. Option C has a wrong syntax and so it is the incorrect answer.

21.B - Topic 103.5

When you append an ampersand to a command the shell starts the command in background. This makes option B the correct answer.

22.A - Topic 103.6

The Linux **niceness scale** goes from -20 to 19. The -20 value corresponds to the highest priority for scheduling, while the 19 value corresponds to the lowest priority for scheduling. So the maximum **nice** value that can be set for a process by a regular user is 19. This makes option A the correct answer.

23.B - Topic 101.2

One of the most common boot parameters that you can pass to the kernel from the boot loader is **init**. This sets the initial command to be executed by the kernel. For example, you can use **init=/bin/sh** to boot to shell. Therefore, option B is the correct answer. The **root** parameter tells the kernel what device is to be used as the root filesystem while booting and this makes option A incorrect. Options C and D contain invalid boot parameters and are therefore incorrect.

24.grub-mkconfig - Topic 102.2

The **grub-mkconfig** command is used to generate a configuration file for GRUB 2. Therefore, once edited **/etc/default/grub**, you have to run this command to generate a new configuration file.

25.B - Topic103.5

The **xeyes** application has stopped running, as indicated by the terminal output message. The number 1 in this message is its job number. This application can be restarted in foreground by typing **fg %1**. In fact, the **fg** command resumes the specified job in foreground and makes it the current job. Therefore, option B is the correct answer. In option D the job number is wrong and so this option is incorrect. The **bg** command is used to run jobs in background and therefore options A and C are incorrect. The **CTRL+Z** keystrokes are used to suspend processes and this makes option E the incorrect answer.

26. B - Topic 103.7

Sed is a stream-oriented editor which uses regular expressions. The **s/pattern1/pattern2/** syntax is used to substitute the first occurrence of **pattern1** with **pattern2** for each line. If you append a letter **g** to the end (**s/pattern1/pattern2/g**), **sed** performs a global substitution. By default, the **sed** command sends the modified text to the standard output. Therefore, option B is the correct answer.

27. A - Topic 103.8

Using **vi** in command mode, the **p** key puts the line or the lines in the buffer into the text after the current line. So, if you press **pp**, the lines in the buffer are inserted twice, making option A the correct answer. Options B, C and D describe the effect of typing **yy**, **dd** and x, respectively, and are therefore incorrect.

28. C - Topic 103.5

The **kill** command is used to send a signal to a process. The basic syntax is **kill PID** and the default signal, if no one is specified, is TERM (15). The 9 and 15 numbers are simply the PIDs of the processes; so option C is the correct answer.

29. A, D, E - Topic 101.3

The -r option of the **shutdown** command is used to reboot the system after shutdown. You can also use the **init** command to switch to runlevel 6, which is reserved for reboots. Finally, a shortcut command named **reboot** can be used to accomplish the same task. Therefore, options A, D and E are the correct answers. The --reboot long option of the **shutdown** command does not exist as well as the **restart** command; so options B and F are incorrect. The **init 0** command tells **init** to switch to runlevel 0 and so it shuts down the system. This makes option C the incorrect answer.

30.C, D - Topic 103.3

In Linux **tar** and **cpio** are two common utilities which can be used to create an archive file and to restore files from such an archive. Therefore, options C and D are the correct answers. For completeness, the **gzip** and **bzip2** commands are used to compress or decompress files, while the **archfile** command is not valid.

31.A - Topic 101.3

/etc/init.d is a directory which contains initialization and termination scripts used by **init** for changing its states. Therefore, option A is the correct answer.

32.B - Topic 101.3

The **systemctl** command is used to control the Systemd system and service manager. The **start** subcommand is used to start (activate) one or more units specified on the command line and so option B is the correct answer. Option D reverses the unit and the subcommand and is therefore incorrect. Option A is specific for **System V** and so it is the incorrect answer. In fact, **System V** startup scripts are usually located under **/etc/init.d** and so, if you want to start services by hand, you can run these scripts with the **start** command. Option C uses the **System V service** command, but it reverses the **apache2** service and the **start** subcommand and is therefore incorrect.

33.C - Topic 101.1

The **lsmod** command is used to show the status of the modules in the Linux Kernel. If you pipe the output of **lsmod** to the **grep** command, you can view if a specific module is currently loaded in the kernel, also showing the other modules that depend on it. So option C is the correct answer. The other options contain invalid commands and are therefore incorrect.

34.A - Topic 103.2

The command simply converts the **hello world** string from uppercase to lowercase. In fact, the output of the **echo** command is piped to the **tr** command that makes this conversion. However, the string is already in lowercase and so no conversion is made. Therefore, the result is still the **hello world** string and option A is the correct answer.

35. D - Topic 103.8

Using **vi**, you can switch in command mode by pressing the **ESC** key. This makes options A, C and E incorrect. The command mode accepts a series of commands such as **:w** that is used to save the file, **:wq** that is used to save the file and quit, **:q!** that is used to discard changes and quit and **ZZ** that is used to save the file and quit. Therefore, option D is the correct answer, while option B is incorrect.

36. A - Topic 104.2

The **fsck** command is used to check and repair a Linux filesystem. The -A option of this command tells **fsck** to check first the root filesystem and then the other filesystems specified for checking in the **/etc/fstab** file. The filesystems are checked in the order specified by the sixth field of this file. Therefore, option A is the correct answer. The **xfs_repair** command is used to repair corrupt or damaged **XFS** filesystems and is not the right command to use. Adding to this, it has not the --all long option. The commands in options B and D are not valid and therefore these options are incorrect.

37. D - Topic 103.7

In regular expressions the **+** meta-character indicates one or more occurrences of the matching item, the **?** meta-character indicates zero or one occurrence of the matching item and the ***** meta-character indicates zero or more occurrences of the matching item. Therefore, option D is the correct answer.

38. B - Topic 104.1

The **swapon** and **swapoff** commands are used to enable and disable paging and swapping on a device. Therefore, once set up a Linux swap area, you need to run the **swapon** command to activate it, making option B the correct answer.

39. B, D - Topic 101.1

Options A, C and E describe correctly what happens if you use the -nn, -b and -t options of the **lspci** command and are therefore the incorrect answers. The -s option is used to show only devices in the specified domain, bus, slot and function, while the -d option is used to show only devices with specified vendor and device ID. This makes option B false and therefore the correct answer. The **lspci** command can display a lot of information about devices, but not the MAC address of the Ethernet network card, making also option D false and therefore correct.

40. C - Topic 103.3

The **mkdir** command is used to create directories. The -p option tells **mkdir** to create parent directories as needed without reporting any errors if a directory already exists. Therefore, option C is the correct answer. The -m option is used to set a file mode for the created directories and so option A is incorrect. The -r and the -a options are not valid for the **mkdir** command and therefore options B and D are the incorrect answers.

41. B - Topic102.4

On a Debian-derived GNU/Linux system, **dpkg** is a package management tool that can install, build, remove and manage packages. You can use the -L (--listfiles) action to list the files installed to your system from a specified package, the -S (--search) action to find which package contains a specified file, the -C (--audit) action to search for partially installed packages and to have a hint on what to do with them and the -l (--list) action to list all installed packages, whose names match a given pattern. Therefore, option B is the correct answer.

42. C - Topic 103.7

The **grep** command is used to print lines matching a pattern. Uncommented lines are lines that do not start with #. The ^ symbol represents the beginning of a line and so option A is incorrect because it finds all commented lines. To reverse the search, you can use the -v option and this makes option C the correct answer.

Option B is used to find non-empty lines, while option D represents another way to find commented lines and therefore these options are incorrect.

43. D - Topic 103.3

The **find** command is used to search for files in a directory hierarchy based on different criteria such as name, size, time stamp and so on. In particular, you can search by file size using the **-size** expression: you can search for files that have a specific size (indicating only the N value) or for files that are either smaller (using -N) or larger (using +N) than a given value. You can use the **-type** expression to restrict the search: for example, you can specify **f** to search for regular files and **d** to search for directories. The **find** command searches for files in the given directory and in all subdirectories and you can refer to the current working directory with a dot. Therefore, the command specified in the question finds all regular files in the current working directory and in all subdirectories larger than 100 bytes in size and so option D is the correct answer.

44. B, C - Topic 104.3

If you want to list all currently mounted filesystems you can display the **/etc/mtab** file or use the **mount** command. In particular, the -l option of the **mount** command adds the labels to this listing. In order to provide a list of all mounted filesystems you can also display the contents of the **/proc/mounts** file. The output of this file is similar to **/etc/mtab**, but is more accurate. Therefore, options B and C are the correct answer. For completeness, the **/etc/fstab** file contains information about the filesystems that the system can mount, while the **mounts** and **lsfs** commands are not valid.

45. C - Topic 103.5

The **watch** command is used to execute a program periodically, showing full-screen output. By default, the program is run every 2 seconds. So you can use **watch** to run the **free** command that is used to display the total amount of free and used memory in the system. This makes option C the correct answer. The **uptime** command is used to display the current time, how long the system has been running, how many users are currently logged on and the system load averages for the past 1, 5 and 15 minutes; therefore, option A is the incorrect answer. In Linux, **screen** and **tmux** are two common terminal multiplexers and so options B and D are incorrect.

46. B, D - Topic 102.2

GRUB Legacy numbers both disks and partitions starting from 0, while GRUB 2 numbers partitions starting from 1 and disks starting from 0. This makes option B correct and options A and C incorrect. Another change in GRUB 2, compared to GRUB Legacy, is that GRUB 2 can boot an operating system from a LVM or RAID disk and therefore also option D is correct. Both Grub Legacy and GRUB 2 can boot a Windows OS and so option E is incorrect.

47. B - Topic 102.5

Using **rpm**, one of the most common operations is uninstalling a package. You can use the -e and --erase options to accomplish this task. Therefore, option B is the correct answer.

48. C - Topic 104.7

According to the Filesystem Hierarchy Standard (FHS), the **/usr/share/doc** directory is the location where you can find most of the Linux documentation. This makes option C the correct answer.

49. D - Topic 104.1

The MBR is 512 bytes and the partition table is in the area at the end (after 440 bytes). So, if you want to erase the entire MBR of a disk, also removing the partition table and the disk signature, you must specify its entire size (512 bytes) in the **dd** command. Otherwise, if you want to wipe out the MBR of a disk, keeping the partition table and the disk signature, you must tell the **dd** command to erase only the first area (440 bytes). Therefore, option D is correct, while option C is incorrect. The **grub-install** command is used to install GRUB to a device and it has not the --erase option; this makes option B the incorrect answer. Option A contains an invalid command and is therefore incorrect.

50. B - Topic 102.6

Virtual Machines run on the same physical server and can have different operating systems. This makes option B correct and option A incorrect. Options C and D describe containers and are therefore incorrect.

51. C - Topic 102.5

The **/etc/yum.repos.d** directory contains the files used by **yum** to locate its repositories. You can add files to this directory if you want to add new repositories to the **yum repository list**. Therefore, option C is the correct answer.

52. D - Topic 102.1

A MBR disk uses up to four primary partitions, one of which can be an extended partition. The extended partition is a special type of primary partition that contains logical partitions. This makes option D the correct answer.

53. nice - Topic 103.6

The **nice** command is used to run a program with an adjusted niceness, which affects process scheduling. The range of possible values spans from -20 (highest priority for scheduling) to 19 (lowest priority for scheduling). If no adjustment value is specified, the **nice** command uses 10 as a default.

54. B - Topic 104.3

The **umount** command is used to unmount a filesystem, by specifying either the mount point or the device name as argument. Therefore, option B is the correct answer. The **unmount** command is not valid and so options C and D are incorrect. The **mount** command is used to mount a filesystem and it has not the -u option; this makes option A the incorrect answer.

55. D - Topic 101.2

In UEFI booting the firmware executes a boot manager that is useful to select which boot loader to launch and then the selected boot loader launches its own kernel. This makes option D the correct answer. The other options describe wrong boot sequences and are therefore incorrect.

56. D - Topic 104.3

The **/etc/fstab** file contains information about the filesystems that the system can mount. Each filesystem is described on a separate six-fields line. The third field describes the type of the filesystem as indicated in option D, that is therefore the correct answer. For completeness, options A, B, C and E describe the fourth, the second, the first and the sixth field of the **/etc/fstab** file.

57. B - Topic 104.5

The **umask** command is used to set the file mode creation mask. This command takes an octal value as argument; if fewer than 4 digits are entered, leading zeros are assumed. The **umask** value of 022 means that any permission (read, write and execute) may be set for the owner and write permission is prohibited for the group and the others. The resulting permissions will be 644 (rw-r--r--) for files and 755 (rwxr-xr-x) for directories. So option B is the correct answer.

58. B - Topic 104.5

The **umask** command is used to get or set the file mode creation mask. If you want to find out your current user mask setting, you can type the **umask** command without any parameters. If you want to change your current user mask setting you can type the **umask** command followed by the new value that you want to set. This operation can also be performed by ordinary users (not only by root) and affects the file mode creation mask of the current shell execution environment. Therefore, option B is the correct answer.

59.A - Topic 104.6

The **ln** command is used to make links between files. The **ln TARGET LINK_NAME** command creates a link to **TARGET** with the name **LINK_NAME**. The **ln** command creates hard links by default, but you can use the -s (--symbolic) option to make symbolic links instead of hard links. Therefore, option A is the correct answer.

60.A - Topic 103.4

In order to redirect the output of a command to a specified file you can use the **>** and **>>** redirection operators. The first creates a new file or overwrites an existing one, while the second creates a new file or appends the output to an existing one. This makes option A correct and option B incorrect. The **&>** and **&>>** operators are similar to **>** and **>>**, except that they redirect both standard output and standard error to the same specified file; so option D is the incorrect answer. Option C contains a wrong command and is therefore incorrect. Anyway, you can use the | operator between two commands to redirect the standard output of the first to the standard input of the second.

Answers to the Practice Exam 2

1. C - Topic 103.4

The command shows an example of redirection, where the standard error is redirected to the current location of the standard output, which is the **report.txt** file. So an error message is written in **report.txt** (because the **view.txt** file does not exist) and this makes option C the correct answer.

2. /usr/share/man - Topic 104.7

According to the FHS, **/usr/share/man** is the location where you can usually find man pages.

3. C - Topic 102.4

On a Debian-derived GNU/Linux system, **dpkg** is a package management tool that can install, build, remove and manage packages. The -l (--list) action is used to list all installed packages whose names match a given pattern. If no pattern is given, all installed packages are listed. The -L (--listfiles) action is used to list the files installed to your system from a specified package; the -S (--search) action is used to find which package contains a specified file and the -C (--audit) action is used to search for partially installed packages and to have a hint on what to do with them. Therefore, option C is the correct answer.

4. B - Topic 103.4

Linux shells use three standard I/O streams: the standard input (stdin) that corresponds to the file descriptor 0, the standard output (stdout) that corresponds to the file descriptor 1 and the standard error (stderr) that corresponds to the file descriptor 2. So, when you use the **2>&1** expression after a command, the standard error is redirected to the current location of the standard output. This makes option B the correct answer.

5. D - Topic 103.6

The Linux **niceness scale** goes from -20 to 19. The -20 value corresponds to the highest priority for scheduling (most favorable scheduling), while the 19 value corresponds to the lowest priority for scheduling (least favorable scheduling). Therefore, option D is the correct answer.

6. D - Topic 103.4

The **noclobber** setting of the **set** built-in command is used to prevent unintentional overwriting of existing files while using I/O redirection on the bash shell. This makes option D the correct answer. The other options contain invalid settings and are therefore incorrect.

7. sha512sum - Topic 103.2

The **sha512sum** command is used to compute and check a SHA512 message digest.

8. B - Topic 102.5

The **yum** main configuration file is **/etc/yum.conf**. This file contains one mandatory **main** section that defines all global configuration options and can also contain one or more **repository** sections that define the configuration for each repository. This makes option B the correct answer.

9. C - Topic 103.8

In command mode, the **vi** editor accepts a series of commands that you can use to perform editing operations and to eventually save and get out of **vi**. For example, you can type **:w** (option A) to save the file, **:q!** (option B) to discard changes and quit, **ZZ** (option C) to save the file and quit and **:!** (option D) to run a shell command. Therefore, option C is the correct answer.

10.D - Topic 102.2

Using GRUB 2, you can find general settings, such as background or timeouts, in the **/etc/default/grub** file. In this file you can set, for example, the **GRUB_TIMEOUT** variable that specifies the time in seconds to wait for keyboard input before booting the default menu entry. Therefore, option D is the correct answer.

11.D - Topic 102.5

Zypper is a command line package manager used for installing, updating and removing packages as well as for managing repositories. The **info** subcommand is used to display detailed information about the specified packages, while the **what-provides** subcommand is used to list packages providing the specified capability. So option D is the correct answer, while option B is incorrect. Options A and C contain invalid subcommands and are therefore incorrect.

12.A - Topic 103.5

In Linux you can use the **kill -l** command to list available signals, each of which has a name and a number. The SIGHUP signal has a numerical value of 1 and this makes option A the correct answer. Options B, C and D contain the numerical value of the SIGQUIT, SIGKILL and SIGTERM signals, respectively, and are therefore incorrect.

13.PATH - Topic 103.1

The **PATH** environment variable contains a list of directory names separated by colons in which the shell looks for commands or programs you run at the command line. So, if you want to add a new directory to this list, you must modify the value of the **PATH** environment variable.

14.D - Topic 104.5

The **chown** command is used to change file owner and group, but only users with root privileges can change the owner of a file. In fact, also the file owner cannot change its ownership, unless the owner is root or uses (if allowed) the **sudo** command to run **chown**. Therefore, option D is the correct answer. For completeness, the **chmod** command, specified in option B, is used to change the permissions of a file.

15.D - Topic 103.7

The **grep** command is used to print lines matching a pattern. The ^ symbol matches the beginning of a line, while the **$** symbol matches the end of a line. So you can use the **^$** regular expression to match empty lines and so option C is incorrect. To reverse the search, you can use the -v option, making option D the correct answer. Options A and B are used to find all lines with or without a dot and are therefore incorrect.

16.D - Topic 102.3

Option D describes correctly the steps to add a new directory to the library path for all users in the system. In fact, first you need to add the new directory to the **/etc/ld.so.conf** file and then you need to run the **ldconfig** command.

17.B - Topic 101.2

When the kernel finishes loading, it runs the initial system program, **/sbin/init**, which is responsible for starting the rest of the system services on a Linux machine. It has Process ID (PID) 1, because it is the first program to run on the system. Therefore, option B is the correct answer.

18.C - Topic 104.1

The **fdisk** command with the -l option is used to list partitions for MBR formatted disks. This makes option C the correct answer. The **mdisk**, **partitions**, **diskls** and **lsdisk** commands are not valid and therefore options A, B, D and E are incorrect.

19. D - Topic 103.5

The **kill** command is used to send a signal to a process and its basic syntax is **kill -s signal PID**, specifying the signal with the name or the number. The TERM, QUIT, STOP and KILL signals have a numerical value of 15, 3, 19 and 9, respectively, and the default signal, if no one is specified, is TERM. Therefore, the command in the question is valid and option D describes its behavior correctly.

20. C - Topic 102.5

On a RPM-based distribution, **rpm** is a Package Manager, which can be used to install, build, query, update, erase and manage packages. You can use the -l and -p options with the -q operation to query and display the files contained in the uninstalled RPM package specified on the command line. Therefore, option C is the correct answer. For completeness, you can use the command in option A to display the files contained in the specified package, the command in option B to display information (including name, version and description) about the specified package and the command in option D to verify the package that owns the specified file.

21. B - Topic 104.2

The **mke2fs** command is used to create an **ext2**, **ext3** or **ext4** filesystem. You can use the -U option to create the filesystem with a specified UUID, the -t option to specify the filesystem type, the -c option to check the device for bad blocks before creating the file system and the -T option to specify how the filesystem is going to be used so that **mke2fs** can choose optimal filesystem parameters for that use. Therefore, option B is the correct answer.

22. renice - Topic 103.6

The **renice** command is used to alter the scheduling priority of one or more running processes. You must have superuser privileges to give your processes higher scheduling priority.

23.A - Topic 103.2

Linux has a variety of commands for working with compressed data. The **zcat**, **bzcat** and **xzcat** commands are used to view the contents of a **gzip**, **bzip2** and **xz** compressed file, respectively, without uncompressing it. These commands expand a compressed file to the standard output so that you can have a look at its contents. The file specified in the question has been compressed with the **gzip** compression program and so **zcat** is the right command to use. If you want to view only the first 100 lines, you have to pipe the output of **zcat** to the **head** command, specifying (through the -n option) the number of lines to view. In fact, **head** is used to output the first part of files, while **tail** is used to output the last part of files. Therefore, option A is the correct answer.

24.C - Topic 103.1

The bash shell maintains a history of the commands you type on the command line. If you want to rerun your most recent command, you can use the **!!** (or **!-1**) command. This makes option C the correct answer. The **!N** command is used to run the Nth history command, while the **!-N** command is used to run the command that is N commands back in the history. Therefore, options A, B and D are incorrect.

25.B - Topic 101.3

In System V each runlevel is a preset operating state that defines what services should be active for that runlevel. Three of those runlevels are reserved for special purposes: **0** that is used to shut down the system, **1** that is used for single-user mode and **6** that is used to reboot the system. The other runlevels have different usages depending on the various distributions. Therefore, option B is the correct answer.

26.A - Topic 101.2

The Linux kernel accepts many boot parameters at the moment it is started. One of these is **root**, which specifies to the kernel what device is to be used as the root filesystem while booting. Therefore, option A is the correct answer. Another common parameter is **rw** that is used to tell the kernel to mount the root filesystem read/write, making option C incorrect. Finally, the **fsroot** and **rootfs** parameters are not valid and so options B and D are the incorrect answers.

27. C - Topic 102.2

In the GRUB Legacy configuration file, you can specify a set of options (or menu commands) that control how GRUB operates. The **default** menu command specifies the GRUB default entry that is loaded if the user does not make a choice within a timeout, while the **timeout** menu command specifies the time (in seconds) that has to expire before the default entry is booted. This makes option C correct and option A incorrect. The **root** and **kernel** options in each menu item specify the partition to boot and the kernel image and parameters to load. Therefore, options B and D are incorrect.

28. A, D - Topic 102.1

The **/etc** and **/dev** directories contain host-specific system configurations and device files, respectively, and so should never be placed on separate partitions. The **/usr** directory contains most Linux program and data files and is commonly split off into a separate partition, as well as the **/home** and **/var** directories that hold user data files and variable data. Therefore, options A and D are the correct answers.

29. C - Topic 104.6

The **ln** command is used to make links between files. The **ln TARGET LINK_NAME** command creates a hard link to **TARGET** with the name **LINK_NAME**. If you want to create a symbolic link instead of a hard link, you can use the -s (--symbolic) option. Therefore, option C is the correct answer.

30. A, C - Topic 102.4

On a Debian-derived GNU/Linux system you can manage packages using the **apt-get** and **dpkg** utilities. In order to remove a specified package, you can use either the **apt-get** command with the **remove** subcommand or the **dpkg** command with the **-r (--remove)** action. In particular, the **dpkg -r** command is used to remove a package leaving configuration files intact. So options A and C are the correct answers. The other options contain invalid commands and are therefore incorrect.

31.B - Topic 103.3

The **cp** command is used to copy files and directories. You must specify one or more source names and one target name. If the target is an existing directory, then all sources are copied into the target. Therefore, option B is the correct answer.

32.A - Topic 104.1

The **mkfs** command is used to build a Linux filesystem on a device, usually a hard disk partition. The -t (--type) option of this command specifies the type of filesystem to be built. If not specified, **mkfs** uses the default filesystem type, which is currently **ext2**. This makes option A the correct answer.

33.C - Topic103.8

Using **vi** in command mode, you can press **yy** to copy the current line into the buffer and **Nyy** (or **yNy**) to copy the next **N** lines, including the current line, into the buffer. This makes option C the correct answer. For completeness, option A deletes eleven lines, beginning with the current line, option B puts the lines in the buffer into the text after the current line eleven times and then another time (totally twelve times) and option D deletes eleven characters, starting with the character under the cursor.

34.A - Topic 101.1

In Linux there are many types of I/O ports (such as serial and parallel ports), each of which corresponds to a specific device name. The first serial port has file name **/dev/ttyS0**, the second serial port has file name **/dev/ttyS1** and so on. This makes option A the correct answer. The numbering of serial ports starts from 0 and therefore option B is incorrect. The device names **/dev/serial0**,

/dev/serial1 and **/dev/serial2** are not valid and so options C and D are incorrect.

35.A - Topic 102.4

On a Debian-derived GNU/Linux system, **apt-get** is the command-line tool for handling packages. The **apt-get update** command is used to re-synchronize the package index files from their sources. The **/etc/apt/sources.list** file tells **apt-get** where to look for packages, specifying the locations (local file system, CD-ROM, HTTP or FTP) from which the indexes of available packages are fetched. You can also add more sources in the **/etc/apt/sources.list.d** directory. An **update** should always be performed before an **upgrade** or **dist-upgrade**, before installing or updating any package, and so always after modifying **/etc/apt/sources.list** or adding files to **/etc/apt/sources.list.d**. This makes option A the correct answer. Options B and C contain invalid commands and are therefore incorrect. The **updatedb** command is used to create or update the database used by **locate** and so option D is incorrect.

36.A - Topic 104.5

The **chmod** command is used to change permissions on a file. The read, write and execute permissions correspond to the bit numbers 4, 2 and 1, respectively. In order to determine the owner permission digit, the group permission digit and the other permission digit, the corresponding permission bit numbers are added up. So the owner permission digit will be 6 (read and write, 4 + 2), the group permission digit will be 4 (read, 4) and the other permission digit will be 0 (no permission for others). Therefore, option A is the correct answer. For completeness, option B represents read and write permissions for the owner and read-only permission for all others, option C represents read and write permissions for the owner and no permission for anyone else and option D represents read, write and execute permissions for the owner and no permission for anyone else.

37.A, C - Topic 101.3

If you want to switch to single user mode, you can use the **telinit** command. It takes a one-character argument and tells **init** to perform a particular action. If you specify 0, 1, 2, 3, 4, 5 or 6 as argument the **telinit** command will tell **init** to switch to the specified runlevel. So you can switch to single user mode by specifying 1 as argument, making option A the correct answer. Using the **telinit** command, you can also specify S or s as argument to accomplish the same task and therefore also option C is correct. The U or u arguments of the **telinit** command are used to tell **init** to re-execute itself (preserving the state) without re-examining the **/etc/inittab** file and so option E is incorrect. The command in option B has a wrong syntax, while the command in option D is not valid; therefore, these options are incorrect.

38.chgrp - Topic 104.5

The **chgrp** command is used to change the group ownership (but not the owner) of one or more files. Instead, if you want to change file owner and group, you can use the **chown** command.

39.C - Topic 104.2

The **xfs_repair** command is used to repair corrupt or damaged **XFS** filesystems. This makes option C the correct answer. The **xfs_metadump** debug tool is used to copy the metadata from an **XFS** filesystem to a file and so option A is incorrect. Options B and D contain invalid commands and are therefore incorrect.

40.C - Topic 103.1

If you want to execute more commands so that each command will execute only if the previous one succeeded (exit code 0), you can combine them using the **&&** operator. Otherwise, if you want to execute more commands so that each command will execute only if the previous one failed (exit code not 0), you can combine them using the || operator. This makes option C correct and option B incorrect. Options A and D have a wrong syntax and are therefore incorrect.

41.C - Topic 103.3

The **ls** command is used to list the contents of a directory. This command is often used in conjunction with wildcard specifications that permit to create a particular pattern, defining a subset of files or directories. Two typical wildcards are: **?** that matches any single character and ***** that matches zero or more characters. Therefore, if you want to list all the **.sh** files in your current working directory, you can use the ***.sh** wildcard expression, as stated in option C that is therefore the correct answer. For completeness, you can use the syntax in option A to list all the **.sh** files with three characters in their name, the syntax in option B to list all files with a two-character extension and the syntax in option D to list all the **.sh** files with only one character in their name.

42.C - Topic 103.7

The **sed** stream editor is used to perform basic text transformations on an input stream. The **s/pattern1/pattern2/** syntax is used to substitute the first occurrence of **pattern1** with **pattern2** for each line. If you append a number N to the end (**s/pattern1/pattern2/N**), **sed** replaces only the Nth occurrence of **pattern1** (with **pattern2**) for each line. The -i option of the **sed** command is used to edit files in place. Therefore, option C is the correct answer.

43.B - Topic 103.4

<< is a valid redirection operator and option B describes its behavior correctly (thus making option D incorrect). Instead, options A and C describe the behavior of the **<** and **<<<** operators, respectively, and are therefore the incorrect answers.

44.A - Topic 103.7

The **sed** command is a stream-oriented editor which uses regular expressions. The **s/pattern1/pattern2/** syntax is used to substitute the first occurrence of **pattern1** with **pattern2** for each line. The **^** symbol matches the starting position of any line and so the **^:** expression matches any line starting with colon. Therefore, the command specified in the question, removes any colon at the beginning of each line and sends the modified text to the standard output. This makes option A the correct answer.

45.B - Topic 103.5

The question assumes you are working with the bash shell. If a task is running in foreground, you can press CTRL+Z to suspend its execution and obtain the control of the terminal. Therefore, option B is the correct answer. For completeness, the CTRL+C keystrokes are used to interrupt the execution of a task (running in foreground), while the CTRL+S and CTRL+R keystrokes are used to search the history forward and backward, respectively.

46.C - Topic 101.3

System V runlevels, which have a special meaning, have a mapping with a specific Systemd target. The **runlevel 0,** which is used to halt the system, matches **runlevel0.target** or **poweroff.target**; the **runlevel 6,** which is used to reboot the system, matches **runlevel6.target** or **reboot.target**; the **runlevel 1** that represents single user mode matches **runlevel1.target** or **rescue.target** and the **emergency runlevel** that represents the emergency shell matches **emergency.target**. Therefore, option C is the correct answer.

47.B - Topic 104.3

Option B describes correctly what happens when you mount a filesystem over an existing directory that already contains files and subdirectories. In fact, these files and subdirectories are not lost (whether you write or not on the device) and are not put in the swap space, but are no longer visible until you unmount the filesystem.

48.D - Topic 104.3

The **/etc/fstab** file contains descriptive information about the filesystems that the system can mount. Each filesystem is described on a separate line and each line has six fields: the filesystem to be mounted, the mount point, the filesystem type, the mount options, the backup operation field and the filesystem check order. The fields on each line are separated by tabs or spaces. Option C specifies five fields for the **/etc/fstab** file, while option B reverses the first and the second field and specifies a wrong mount option (the **nouser** option do not allow ordinary users to mount the filesystem). So these two options are incorrect. The fields in options A and D are in the right order, but option A uses the **nouser** option that makes it the incorrect answer. In fact, the right mount option to use is **user** that allows ordinary users to mount the filesystem and only the user who mounted the filesystem can unmount it. Therefore, option D is the correct answer.

49. A - Topic 102.6

Option A describes one the most important benefits you can have using container technology. In fact, with the OS (Operation System) virtualization, you have a fast startup and a small overhead and therefore option A is the correct answer. Containers are very light as indicated in option B, but using this technology, you can only have a single OS instance with multiple workloads, making option B incorrect. Option C describes a feature of virtual machines, while option D describes exactly the opposite of what happens with containers. So these two options are incorrect.

50. A - Topic 103.8

Using **vi** in command mode, you can press the **j** key to move the cursor down one line, the **k** key to move the cursor up one line, the **h** key to move the cursor left one character and the **l** key to move the cursor right one character. You can type a number **N** before one of these keys to move the cursor down or up of **N** lines and left of right of **N** characters. So option A contains the right combination keys to move the cursor right ten characters and then down five lines and is therefore the correct answer. For completeness, you can use the combination keys in option B to move the cursor right ten characters and then up five lines, the combination keys in option C to move the cursor left ten characters and then down five lines and the combination keys in option D to move the cursor left ten characters and then up five lines.

51. E - Topic 104.6

The command specified in the question tries to create a hard link to a directory. This operation is not allowed: in fact, you cannot create hard links to directories because they would break the filesystem structure, creating directory loops. The **ln** command with the -d (--directory) option allows the superuser to attempt to create hard links to directories, but it will probably fail due to system restrictions, even for the superuser. You should use symbolic links instead of hard links. Therefore, option E is the correct answer.

52. A, C - Topic 103.3

The **touch** command is used to update access and modification times of specified files to the current time. Therefore, option C is the correct answer. The command in option A is an example of redirection that appends the **EOF** string to the existing file named **report.txt** in the current working directory. As result, this command updates the modify timestamp of the specified file and so also option A is the correct answer. The **file** command is used to determine the file type, while the **cat** command is used to concatenate files, or standard input, to standard output. These two commands do not update the modify timestamp of the specified file, making options B and D the incorrect answer. The **timeupdate** command is not valid and therefore option E is incorrect.

53. D - Topic 101.2

If you want to modify kernel parameters or add new ones, on the GRUB2 menu you can select and edit (by pressing the **e** key) the entry that you want to modify and then locate and edit the line starting with **linux**. One of the most common parameters that is passed from the boot loader to the kernel is the word **single** that is used to boot the computer in single user mode, for example, for rescue operations. Therefore, option D is the correct answer.

54. D, E - Topic 104.7

According to the FHS, files can be shareable or unshareable and static or variable. Shareable files can be shared between computers, while unshareable files must reside on the system on which they are used. Static files normally change only through the direct intervention of the system administrator, while variable files may be changed by users, scripts and system processes. Based on these file distinctions, the **/etc** and **/boot** directories contain static and unshareable files, the **/usr** and **/opt** directories contain static and shareable files and the **/var/mail** directory contains variable and shareable files. This makes options D and E the correct answers.

55. C - Topic 103.5

The **nohup** command is used to start another command (in background or in foreground) immune to hangups and to append standard output and standard error to a file. If standard output is a terminal, **nohup** appends the output to the **nohup.out** file and if standard error is a terminal, **nohup** redirects it to the standard output. Then, if the **nohup.out** file cannot be written to, the standard output and the standard error are appended to the **$HOME/nohup.out** file and if that file cannot be written to, the command is not run. Therefore, option C is the correct answer. The **fg** command is used to continue a stopped job by running it in foreground and this makes option A incorrect. The commands in options B, D and E are not valid and so these options are incorrect.

56. A - Topic 103.1

The **set** built-in command, without options or arguments, displays the names and values of all shell variables and functions. You can also combine it with the **grep** utility to filter the output. This makes option A the correct answer. The other options contain invalid commands and are therefore incorrect.

57. A - Topic 104.3

The **/etc/fstab** file contains information about the filesystems that the system can mount, while the **/etc/mtab** file contains information about all currently mounted filesystems. So option A is the correct answer, while option B is incorrect. Options C, D and E contain invalid file names and are therefore incorrect.

58. D - Topic 101.1

Both the **modprobe** and **insmod** commands are used to load modules, but **modprobe** is more clever because it loads not only a single module like **insmod,** but all those on which it depends. Therefore, option D is the correct answer, while option B is incorrect. These two command are valid, not deprecated and can be used in all distributions, making options A and C incorrect.

59. A - Topic 103.3

Whenever your file names contain special characters (such as $), you need to escape them with a backslash or protect them with single quotes. Therefore, option A is the correct answer.

60. A - Topic 102.1

The extended partition is a special type of primary partition that contains logical partitions. The MBR partitioning system uses up to four primary partitions, one of which can be an extended partition. Therefore, MBR disks hold at most one extended partition and option A is the correct answer.

Answers to the Practice Exam 3

1. **D - Topic 103.2**

   The **cut** command is used to print selected parts of lines from a specified file to standard output. The **/etc/passwd** file is a colon-separated file that stores account information of each user in the system. Therefore, if you want to use the **cut** command with this file, you have to specify the delimiter, using the -d option. This makes options A and B incorrect. Option C extracts from the first to the fifth field of each line from **/etc/passwd**, while option D extracts the first field and from the third to the fifth field of each line from the same specified file, also using the delimiter. Therefore, option D is the correct answer, while option C is incorrect.

2. **B - Topic 101.3**

   The **runlevel** command is used to print both the previous and the current system runlevel on the standard output, separated by a single space. If the previous runlevel does not exist, the letter **N** is printed instead of the number. So the current runlevel is number 5 and the previous one is number 3. Therefore, option B is the correct answer.

3. **B - Topic 103.1**

   If you want to execute more commands so that each command will execute only if the previous one failed (exit code not 0), you can combine them using the || operator. If you want to run more commands in sequence regardless of whether the previous ones failed or not, you can separate them with semicolons. If you want to pipe more commands so that the standard output of the previous one is

used as the standard input of the next, you can combine them using the |
redirection operator. So option B is the correct answer, while options C and D are
incorrect. Option A has a wrong syntax and is therefore incorrect.

4. A - Topic 103.1

You can usually find your bash history in the **.bash_history** file in your home
directory. In general, when the shell starts up, the history is initialized from the
file named by the **HISTFILE** variable (by default **~/.bash_history**). Therefore,
option A contains the right statement and is the correct answer.

5. B - Topic 102.2

GRUB Legacy numbers both disks and partitions starting from 0. In **root (hd0,6)**
the number 0 refers to hard drives, while the number 6 refers to partitions. So
the system is on partition 7 of the first hard drive and the device name is
/dev/hda7. Therefore, option B is the correct answer.

6. D - Topic 104.6

Hard links are directory entries that point to the same inode. When you delete
the original file the hard link will still exist, making option D the correct answer
and options B and C incorrect. Option A contains a wrong statement and is
therefore incorrect.

7. A - Topic 103.7

The **sed** command is a stream-oriented editor which uses regular expressions.
The -r option of this command tells **sed** to use extended regular expressions
rather than basic regular expressions; the -e option is used to combine multiple
commands and the -i option is used to specify that files are to be edited in-place.
So option A is the correct answer, while options B and C are incorrect. Options D
and E contain invalid long options for the **sed** command and are therefore
incorrect.

8. A, C - Topic 104.5

The **chown** command is used to change file owner and group. The -R option and the --recursive long option of this command are used to operate recursively, making options A and C the correct answers. The -f option is used to suppress most error messages and this makes option E incorrect. Options B and D are not valid and are therefore incorrect.

9. D - Topic 104.5

The directory has the sticky bit set. It is represented symbolically by the **t** and **T** characters in the place of the executable flag for other users (the last character). The lowercase **t** and uppercase **T** appear when the execute bit for others permissions is set or not set, respectively. In the octal format, the sticky bit has the value 1 in the first high order digit. The read, write, and execute permissions correspond to the bit numbers 4, 2 and 1, respectively. In order to determine the owner permission digit, the group permission digit and the other permission digit, the corresponding permission bit numbers are added up. So the owner permission digit will be 7 (read, write and execute, 4 + 2 + 1), the group permission digit will be 5 (read and execute, 4 + 1) and the other permission digit will be 5 (read and execute, 4 + 1). Therefore, option D is the correct answer.

10. E - Topic 101.2

The **/proc/cmdline** file contains the parameters passed to the kernel at the time it is started. Therefore, option E is the correct answer.

11. B, C - Topic 104.2

The **tune2fs** command is used to adjust various tunable filesystem parameters on the specified **ext2**, **ext3** or **ext4** filesystem. The -l option of this command is used to list the contents of the filesystem superblock, including the current values of the parameters that **tune2fs** can set (mount count, check interval and so on). This makes option C the correct answer. The **dumpe2fs** command is used to print the superblock and blocks group information for the filesystem present on the specified device and the -h option of this command is used to display only the superblock information. Therefore, also option B is the correct answer. For completeness, the **e2label** command is used to display or change the filesystem label on the **ext2**, **ext3** or **ext4** filesystem located on the specified device, while the **sblock2fs** and **e2superblock** commands are not valid. So options D, A and E are incorrect.

12. D - Topic 103.4

In Linux shells the standard input (stdin) corresponds to the file descriptor 0, the standard output (stdout) corresponds to the file descriptor 1 and the standard error (stderr) corresponds to the file descriptor 2. When you use the **2>1** expression after a command, the standard error is redirected (**>**) to a file named **1**. If you put an ampersand before **1**, the expression assumes a different meaning: in this case, the standard error is redirected to the current location of the standard output. Therefore, option D is the correct answer.

13. /etc/inittab - Topic 101.3

The **/etc/inittab** configuration file describes how the init process should set up the system in a certain run-level. Each line consists of four colon-delimited fields: the ID (Identification Code), the runlevel, the action to be taken and the process to run. For example, the line with the **initdefault** action specifies the runlevel to enter after system boot. Therefore, on a System V-based system, if you want to change the default runlevel, you have to identify and edit the line with the **initdefault** action in the **/etc/inittab** file.

14. A - Topic 103.6

The **nice** command is used to run a program with an adjusted niceness, which affects process scheduling. In order to specify an adjustment nice value of **N**, you can use the -n (or --adjustment=N) option or you can specify the adjustment value preceded by a dash. Therefore, the command in the question specifies an adjustment value of 8 and so the script is run in background at a nice level of 8. This makes option A the correct answer.

15.D - Topic 104.1

FAT (File Allocation Table) is a very portable filesystem and so it is the ideal candidate for being the filesystem for USB drives. In order to format a partition as a particular filesystem type you can use the **mkfs** command. This command is a front end to several filesystem-specific commands: for example, you can use **mkfs.ext3** for **ext3** filesystems, **mkfs.ext4** for **ext4** filesystems and **mkfs.vfat** or **mkfs.msdos** for **FAT** filesystems (both **mkfs.vfat** and **mkfs.msdos** are usually symbolic links to the **mkdosfs** command). Therefore, option D is the correct answer. The -t option of the **mkfs** command is used to specify the type of filesystem to be built, but the **VFAT** (uppercase) specification is not valid (you should use **vfat**). This makes option A incorrect. Options B and C contain invalid commands and are therefore the incorrect answers.

16.D - Topic 103.5

All applications have stopped running as indicated by the terminal output message. Job 4 has a plus sign (+) beside the job number, indicating that it is the current job. This job comes to foreground or background if no job specification is given with the **fg** or **bg** commands. Therefore, option D is the correct answer.

17.C - Topic 102.6

IaaS (Infrastructure as a Service) is a cloud model in which a provider hosts the typical infrastructure components (such as servers, storage, networking hardware) and the hypervisor layer. It also provides a range of useful services such as backup, monitoring, log access and so on. This makes option C the correct answer. Option A describes a **SaaS** (Software as a Service) model; option B describes a **PaaS** (Platform as a Service) model and option D describes a typical scenario for a company that does not concern the **IaaS** model. Therefore, these options are incorrect.

18.B - Topic 102.5

On a RPM-based distribution, **rpm** is a Package Manager, which can be used to install, build, query, update, erase and manage packages. You can use the -a (--all) option with the -V (--verify) operation to verify all packages and the -a option with the -q (--query) operation to query all packages. Therefore, option B is the correct answer, while option A is incorrect. The -v option, normally used with the -i, -U and -F operations, is used to print verbose information during the routine progress and so options C and D are incorrect.

19.C - Topic 102.1

The **/var** directory holds variable data such as system logging files, mail and printer spool directories, transient and temporary files and is commonly split off into a separate partition. The **/usr** directory contains static data and, like **/var**, can be considered for a separate partition. The **/etc** and **/lib** directories contain host-specific system configurations and essential shared libraries and kernel modules, respectively, and so must be on the root partition, because they are vital for the boot process. Therefore, option C is the correct answer.

20.C - Topic 103.5

The CTRL+Z keystrokes are used to suspend a process by sending it the SIGSTOP signal, while the CTRL+C keystrokes are used to interrupt a process by sending it the SIGINT signal. In the bash shell, if the controlling terminal closes or the user logs off, the shell sends a SIGHUP signal to the applications that will likely close. According to this, in order to suspend a foreground task and to resume it in background, first you must press CTRL+Z and then you must run the **bg** command. Therefore, option C is the correct answer.

21.D - Topic102.4

On a Debian-derived GNU/Linux system, **dpkg** is a package management tool that can install, build, remove and manage packages. You can use the -S (--search) action to find which package contains a specified file, the -P (--purge) action to remove a package, including configuration files, the -L (--listfiles) action to list the files installed to your system from a specified package and the -i action (--install) to install a package. Therefore, option D is the correct answer.

22. B - Topic 103.8

Using **vi** in command mode, you can press the **0** key (option A) to move the cursor at the beginning of the current line, the **$** key (option B) to move the cursor at end of the current line, the **o** key (option C) to enter in insert mode in a new line below the current line and the **O** key (option D) to enter in insert mode in a new line above the current line. This makes option B the correct answer.

23. B - Topic 103.4

The **tee** command reads from standard input and sends its output both to standard output and to one or more files. The -a option tells **tee** not to overwrite, but to append to the specified files. According to this, the result of the **date** command is sent to the standard output and appended to the file named **date_time**. This makes option B the correct answer.

24. B - Topic 104.2

The **tune2fs** command allows the system administrator to adjust various tunable filesystem parameters on Linux **ext2**, **ext3** or **ext4** filesystems. The -c option is used to adjust the number of mounts after which the filesystem will be checked by **e2fsck**. If the value is 0 or -1, the number of times the filesystem is mounted will be disregarded by **e2fsck** and the kernel. The -C option is used to set the number of times the filesystem has been mounted. If the value is greater than the parameter set by the -c option, the **e2fsck** will check the filesystem at the next reboot. Therefore, option B is the correct answer, while option A is incorrect. For completeness, the -E option is used to set extended options for the filesystem, the -e option is used to change the behavior of the kernel code when errors are detected and the --ext-mounts long option is not valid. This makes options C, D and E the incorrect answers.

25. D - Topic 104.1

Common type codes of MBR partitions are: **0x05** (option A), which refers to an old type of extended partition, **0x0f** (option B), which refers to a newer type of extended partition, **0x82** (option C), which refers to a Linux swap partition and

0x83 (option D), which refers to a Linux native filesystem. Therefore, option D is the correct answer.

26. B - Topic 103.1

In the bash shell the **HISTSIZE** variable contains the number of commands to remember in the command history. Therefore, option B is the correct answer.

27. B - Topic 101.1

Under the **/proc** filesystem you can find some important files that can give you useful hardware information: **/proc/ioports** that holds information about I/O ports, **/proc/interrupts** that holds information about IRQs and **/proc/dma** that holds information about DMA channels in use. Therefore, option B is the correct answer.

28. C - Topic 102.1

In Linux **/dev/hda1** represents the first primary partition of the primary master on the primary IDE controller, **/dev/hdb1** represents the first primary partition of the primary slave on the primary IDE controller, **/dev/hdc1** represents the first primary partition of the secondary master on the secondary IDE controller and **/dev/hdd1** represents the first primary partition of the secondary slave on the secondary IDE controller. This makes option C the correct answer.

29. B, C - Topic 103.3

The name of the file you want to decompress contains special characters (two spaces) and so you need to escape them with a backslash or protect them with single quotes. In order to decompress your **.bz2** file, you can use the **bunzip2** and **bzip2 -d** (**--decompress**) commands. Therefore, options B and C are the correct answers.

30. B - Topic 102.2

The **grub-install** command is used to install GRUB Legacy to a device. With GRUB2 you can use **grub-install** or **grub2-install** according to your system. Therefore, option B is the correct answer.

31. A - Topic 103.7

In extended regular expressions some meta-characters such as **?**, **+** or ***** have a special meaning, while in basic regular expressions they are treated as literal characters. If you want to use the special functions of these characters in basic regular expressions, you have to escape them with a backslash. This makes option A correct and option B incorrect. Option C is true for extended regular expressions, but is false for basic regular expressions and so it is the incorrect answer. In extended regular expressions you can treat meta-characters as literal characters by escaping them with a backslash and therefore option D is incorrect.

32. lsusb - Topic 101.1

The **lsusb** command is used to obtain information about USB devices. In order to obtain extended information, you can use the -v option that tells **lsusb** to be verbose.

33. D - Topic 104.3

The **lsof** command is used to check what files are open or what processes have open files on the filesystem you want to unmount and so option D is the correct answer. The **file** command is used to determine file type, making option B incorrect. Options A and C contain invalid commands and are therefore incorrect.

34. C - Topic 104.7

The **/usr/local** hierarchy is intended for use by the system administrator when installing software locally. It is a safe area that is not overwritten when the system software is updated. This directory contains the **/usr/local/bin** subdirectory that is normally considered a good place in which to keep self-compiled or third-party programs. The **/usr/sbin** directory contains programs for administering the system, which can be run only by users with root privileges. The **/usr/share** directory contains architecture-independent data files (such as documents, fonts, icons) and is not normally part of a user's **$PATH.** The **/usr/programs/common/share** directory is not a standard directory according to the FHS and so, like **/usr/share**, it is not normally part of a user's **$PATH**. This makes option C the correct answer.

35. C - Topic 103.1

In the bash shell, double quotes evaluate the variables between them and display their value. Instead, single quotes literally display what is between them without expanding the variables. So the command specified in the question literally echoes what is between single quotes without expanding the **USER** variable. Therefore, option C is the correct answer.

36. C - Topic 103.5

The **ps** command is used to report a snapshot of the current processes. According to the BSD syntax, you can use the **ps aux** command to see every process on the system, while, according to the standard syntax, you can use the **ps -e** (or **ps -A**) command to achieve the same goal. Therefore, option C is the correct answer. The **ps au** command is used to only list all processes with a terminal (according to the BSD syntax) and so option A is incorrect. The -a option of the **ps** command is used to select all processes except both session leaders and processes not associated with a terminal, while the -l option is used to display information using the long format. This makes options B and D the incorrect answers.

37. B, D - Topic 104.3

The **/etc/fstab** file contains descriptive information about the filesystems that the system can mount. Each filesystem is described on a separate six-fields line. The fourth field describes the mount options associated with the filesystem and it is formatted as a comma-separated list of options. The **user** option is used to allow ordinary users to mount the filesystem and only the user who mounted the filesystem can unmount it. The **users** option is similar to **user**, except that any user can unmount the filesystem once it's been mounted. The **nouser** option does not allow ordinary users to mount the filesystem. This makes options B and D correct and option E incorrect. The **owners** and **allow_users** options are not valid and therefore options A and C are incorrect.

38. C, D - Topic 103.5

The **jobs** command is used to find out what jobs are running in the current shell and the -l option of this command is used to also list their PIDs, making option D the correct answer. The **ps** command is used to report a snapshot of the current processes, showing a lot of useful information, including their PIDs. Therefore, also option C is the correct answer. The **free** command is used to display the amount of free and used memory in the system and so option E is incorrect. Options A and B contain invalid commands and are therefore incorrect.

39. A - Topic 103.8

Using the **vi** editor in command mode, you can type **/home** or **?home** to search forward or backward for occurrences of the **home** string in your text. Then you can press **n** or **N** to move to next or to the previous occurrence of your search string. This makes option A correct, while option B incorrect. Option C is used to search forward for occurrences of the **?home** string, while option D is used to search backward for occurrences of the **/home** string. Therefore, these options are incorrect.

40. C - Topic 102.5

On a RPM-based distribution, **rpm** is a Package Manager, which can be used to install, build, query, update, erase and manage packages. The -i (--install) operation is used to install a new package, the -U (--upgrade) operation is used to install a new package or to upgrade an existing one and the -F (--freshen) operation is used to upgrade packages, but only ones for which an earlier version is installed. They are generally used in conjunction with the -v (--verbose) and -h (--hash) options to have a nicer display during the progress of the operation. Therefore, option C is the correct answer.

41.D - Topic 101.2

EFI-based computers read a boot loader file (with .efi extension) from a filesystem on a special partition, known as the EFI System Partition (ESP). The ESP uses the FAT filesystem and stores a separate boot loader for each operating system on the computer. This makes option D correct and options B and C incorrect. For completeness, option A is true for BIOS-based computers, but it does not concern EFI boot loader principles.

42.B - Topic 104.7

The **updatedb** command is used to create or update the database used by **locate**. If the database already exists, its data is reused to avoid rereading directories that have not changed. So, after launching the **updatedb** command, **locate** will also find the newly created files. This makes option B correct and option C incorrect. The **apt-get update** command is used to re-synchronize the package index files from their sources, while the **dbupdate** command is not valid. Therefore, options A and D are incorrect.

43.D - Topic 103.3

The question shows an example of command substitution that is used to allow the output of a command to replace the command itself. For example, through substitution the output of a command can be used as arguments to another command or to set a variable. Command substitution occurs when a command is enclosed as follows: **$(command)** or **`command`**. So the **find** command searches for all the regular **.sh** files in the current directory and in all subdirectories and then its output is used as arguments to the **cp** command. As result, the output files of **find** are copied to the **/tmp** directory, making option D the correct answer.

44.A, C - Topic 103.4

Two common redirection operators are those shown in options A and C: the first (**&>**) is used to redirect both standard output and standard error to the same specified file, while the second (**>>**) is used to redirect the output of a command, creating a new file or appending the output to an existing one. Options B and E contain Boolean operators and are therefore incorrect: in fact, the **&&** operator provides a logical **AND**, while the **||** operator provides a logical **OR**. The **&** operator is used to make a command run in background and so option D is the incorrect answer.

45. E - Topic 103.6

The **nice** command is used to run a program with an adjusted niceness, which affects process scheduling. The range of possible values spans from -20 (most favorable scheduling) to 19 (least favorable scheduling). An ordinary user must have root privileges to specify negative adjustments. So the minimum nice value that can be set for a process by a regular user is 0 (that is also the default nice value for a program that runs without **nice**). Therefore, option E is the correct answer.

46. A - Topic 102.4

On a Debian-derived GNU/Linux system **apt-get** is the command-line tool for handling packages. It has several subcommands such as **remove** that is used to remove a package and **autoremove** that is used to remove a package along with the dependencies that were installed with that package and are no longer used by anything else on the system. Therefore, option A is the correct answer, while option D is incorrect. On Debian-based systems **apt-cache** performs a variety of operations on APT's package cache, but it has not the **remove, autoremove** and **delete** subcommands. This makes options B, C and E incorrect.

47. A, B - Topic 104.6

Hard links are directory entries that point to the same inode and they must reside on a single filesystem. This makes options A and B the correct answers. The operation of creating hard links to directories is usually not allowed, because it would break the filesystem structure creating directory loops. Therefore, option A is incorrect. When you delete the original file the hard link will not become a broken link and it will not be deleted, but it will still exist, making options D and E the incorrect answers.

48.D - Topic 103.8

The **EDITOR** environment variable contains the command that some programs launch when they need to call a text editor. So, if you want to set your favorite text editor, you can change and export this environment variable, making option D the correct answer. For completeness, option A assigns the string **EDITOR** to the **vi** variable and exports it, while options B and C try to set invalid options for the bash built-in **set** command.

49.D - Topic 103.2

The **split** command is used to split a file into fixed-size pieces, creating output files that contain consecutive sections of the file specified as input. By default, the **split** command puts 1000 lines of the specified file into each output file, but the number of lines can be modified using the -l option. The names of the output files consist of a prefix followed by a group of letters: **aa**, **ab**, **ac** and so on. The default prefix is **x**. So, the command specified in the question splits the **foo** file, which has 110 lines, into 5 output files, putting 25 lines into each output file. As result, the files **xaa** of 25 lines, **xab** of 25 lines, **xac** of 25 lines, **xad** of 25 lines and **xae** of 10 lines will be created. Therefore, option D is the correct answer.

50.B - Topic 103.7

In regular expressions the | meta-character is used to separate two possible values. For example, the **10 | ten** expression matches either **10** or **ten**. The | meta-character must be escaped with a backslash in order to be treated as a literal character. Therefore, option B is the correct answer. For completeness, option A describes the meaning of the . meta-character, while option C describe the meaning of the \b position anchor.

51.C - Topic 101.2

During the boot process you can tell Systemd to boot to a specific target by passing the **systemd.unit=** parameter to the kernel. The old System V runlevel 1, which represents single user mode, matches the **rescue.target** or **runlevel1.target** in Systemd. So, if you want to boot in single user mode, you can pass the **systemd.unit=rescue.target** parameter to the kernel as stated in option C that is therefore the correct answer.

52. B - Topic 102.5

Zypper and **yum** are two of the most popular Linux package managers. Both have a set of subcommands including **search**, that is used to find packages, matching any of the given search strings. Therefore, option B is the correct answer.

53. C - Topic 103.4

Option C describes the effect of the command correctly: in fact, the standard output of the **foobar** command is forwarded to the standard input of the **barfoo** command. In general, the pipe (|) operator between two commands is used to redirect the standard output of the first to the standard input of the second.

54. B - Topic 102.4

On a Debian derived GNU/Linux system the **dpkg-reconfigure** command is used to reconfigure a package after it has already been installed. You must pass to the command the name of the package you want to reconfigure and then **dpkg-reconfigure** will ask configuration questions, much like when the package was installed for the first time. This makes option B the correct answer. Options A and E contains invalid commands and are therefore incorrect. The **apt-get** and **apt-cache** commands have not the **reconfigure** subcommand and so options C and D are the incorrect answers.

55. B - Topic 102.3

The **ldd** command is used to print the shared libraries required by each program or shared object specified on the command line. The **ldconfig** command is used to create the necessary links and cache to the most recent shared libraries found in the directories specified on the command line, in the **/etc/ld.so.conf** file and in the trusted directories (**/lib** and **/usr/lib** or **/lib64** and **/usr/lib64**). This makes option B correct and option D incorrect. The commands in options A, C and E are invalid and therefore these options are incorrect.

56. C - Topic 104.3

The **mount** command is used to mount a filesystem. The basic form of this command takes two parameters: the device that contains the filesystem to be mounted and the mount point. If you want to remount an already mounted filesystem, it is not necessary to specify both the device and the mount point, but only one of these two parameters. The question assumes you have already mounted the filesystem and so you can use the **mount** command with either the device or the mount point. This makes option C the correct answer. The -t option of the **mount** command is used to indicate the filesystem type, but option D specifies and invalid one and is therefore incorrect. Finally, option B uses a wrong mount point and option A specifies an invalid command and so these options are incorrect.

57. C - Topic 103.3

The **dd** command is suitable for burning an **iso image** to a USB drive. In fact, this command is used to copy a file, converting and formatting according to the operands. Therefore, option C is the correct answer.

58. A - Topic 101.3

Systemd uses system-state **targets**, which are equivalent to **runlevels**. The default target is defined in **/etc/systemd/system/default.target.** This file is used when the Linux system boots and is normally a symbolic link to the standard target unit file currently set. For example, it can be a symbolic link to the **graphical.target** file in the **/lib/systemd/system/** directory. Therefore, option A is the correct answer.

59.B - Topic 104.5

Option B describes correctly what happens if a directory has the sticky bit set: in fact, the files in the directory can be deleted only by their owners, the directory's owner and root.

60.C - Topic 103.3

The **tar** command is used to create an archive file and to restore files from such an archive. A **.tar** file is often compressed after being created, changing its extension in **.tar.gz**, **.tar.bz2** and **.tar.xz** if you use **gzip**, **bzip2** and **xz**, respectively. If you want to extract files from the compressed archive named **archive.tar.gz**, you can use the **tar** command with the -xzvf options. In fact, the -x option extracts files from the specified archive, the -z option filters the archive through **gzip**, the -f option specifies file input, rather than stdin and the -v option lists files processed verbosely. This makes option C the correct answer. The **zcat** command is used to view the contents of a compressed file without uncompressing it and the **tar** command with the -tvf options is used to list the contents of a tar archive. Therefore, options D and A are incorrect. The **tar** command has not the --gzip-extract and --file-name long options and so option B is incorrect.

Answers to the Practice Exam 4

1. **C - Topic 103.1**

   The **uname** command is used to print system information. With no options or with the -s (--kernel-name) option this command prints the kernel name. Otherwise, you can use the -n (--nodename) option to print the network node hostname, the -r (--kernel-release) option to print the kernel release, the -v (--kernel-version) option to print the kernel version, the -m (--machine) option to print the machine hardware name, the -p (--processor) option to print the processor type or unknown, the -i (--hardware-platform) option to print the hardware platform or unknown, the -o (--operating-system) option to print the operating system and the -a (--all) option to print all information except omit the processor type and the hardware platform if unknown. This makes option C the correct answer. Options A, B, D and E contain invalid commands and are therefore incorrect.

2. **C - Topic 103.4**

   The **&>** redirection operator is used to redirect both standard output and standard error to the same specified file. This makes option C the correct answer.

3. **C, D - Topic 103.5**

   The **ps** command is used to report a snapshot of the current processes also showing their PIDs. You can define the output format you prefer, choosing which information to display (nice value, PID, PPID, command and so on). This makes option C the correct answer. The **top** command is used to provide a dynamic real time view of a running system, displaying system summary information as well as a list of processes currently being managed by the Linux kernel. By default, this command shows the nice value, but the information displayed and their order are all user configurable and the preferred configuration can be made persistent across restarts. Therefore, also option D is correct. The **jobs** command is used to find out what jobs are running in the current shell, while the **nice** command is used to print the default niceness and to run a program with modified scheduling priority. These two commands do not display the nice value of the processes running in the terminal, making options B and A incorrect. Option E contains an invalid command and is therefore incorrect.

4. D - Topic 103.5

The CTRL+C keystrokes are used to interrupt a process immediately by sending it the SIGINT signal. In Linux you can use the **kill -l** command to list all available signals and their matching numerical value. The SIGINT signal matches number 2. This makes option D the correct answer.

5. B - Topic 104.5

There are three special permissions that are available for executable files and directories: Set User ID (SUID), Set Group ID (SGID) and the sticky bit. The SUID permission is assigned to a file and allows the file in which is set to be executed with the privileges of the owner. This permission is symbolically represented by the **s** or **S** character in the place of the executable flag for the owner, if respectively the execute bit for the owner of the file is set or not set. The SGID permission can be assigned to a file or to a directory. If set on a file, it allows the file to be executed with the privileges of the group; if set on a directory, a file created in the directory would inherit the same group of the directory and not the group of the user who had created the file. This permission is symbolically represented by the **s** or **S** character in the place of the executable flag for the group, if respectively the execute bit for the group is set or not set. The sticky bit can be assigned to a directory and it allows the files in the directory to be deleted only by their owners, the directory' s owner and root. It is symbolically represented by the **t** or **T** character in the place of the executable flag for other users (the last character), if respectively the execute bit for others permissions is set or not set. The file specified in the question is owned by root and it has the

SUID permission set; so ordinary users can run the **foo** command and it would always be executed with root privileges. This makes option B the correct answer.

6. A - Topic 102.4

On a Debian-derived GNU/Linux system **dpkg** is a package management tool that can install, build, remove and manage packages. You can use the -P (--purge) action to remove a package, including configuration files, the -p (--print-avail) action to display information about an installed package, the -r (--remove) action to remove a package leaving configuration files and the -C (--audit) action to search for partially installed packages and to have a hint on what to do with them. Therefore, option A is the correct answer.

7. B - Topic 104.7

The **whereis** command is used to locate the binary, source and manual page files for a specified command. You can restrict your search using the -b option to look only for binaries, the -s option to look only for sources and the -m option to look only for manual sections. Therefore, option B is the correct answer. For completeness, the **which** command is used to search for your path for the command you type listing the complete path to the first match it finds, the **locate** command is used to find a file by name and the **search** command is not valid.

8. D - Topic 103.8

Using the **vi** editor in command mode, you can type **/string** or **?string** to search forward or backward for occurrences of **string** in your text. Then you can type **n** to move to next occurrence of **string** and **N** to move to the previous one. Therefore, option D is the correct answer.

9. /etc/mtab - Topic 104.3

The **/etc/mtab** file holds information about all currently mounted filesystems. This file has a format similar to the **/etc/fstab** file that contains information about the filesystems that the system can mount. Therefore, the **/etc/mtab** file can include manually mounted filesystems not listed in **/etc/fstab**.

10. A, B - Topic 101.3

The **telinit** command is strictly related to **/sbin/init**. In fact, you can use the **telinit 0**, **telinit 1**, **telinit 2**, **telinit 3**, **telinit 4**, **telinit 5** or **telinit 6** commands to tell **init** to switch to the specified runlevel, the **telinit Q** or **telinit q** commands to tell **init** to re-examine the **/etc/inittab** file, the **telinit U** or **telinit u** commands to tell **init** to re-execute itself without re-examining the **/etc/inittab** file (preserving the state) and the **telinit S** or **telinit s** commands to tell **init** to switch to single user mode. Therefore, options A and B are the correct answers.

11. C - Topic 103.2

The **tail** command is used to output the last part of files and is very useful for monitoring a log file that is growing. In fact, the -f option tells **tail** to output the last part (10 lines by default) of a log file and to monitor it for updates so that **tail** continues to output any new line that is added to the log file. This makes option C the correct answer. You can use the -n option to specify the number of the last lines to output (instead of the default 10), the -c option to specify the number of the last bytes to output and the -v option to always print headers (giving file names). Therefore, options A, B and D are incorrect.

12. D - Topic 103.1

In the bash shell the **HISTFILE** variable contains the name of the file to which the command history is saved. The default value is **~/.bash_history**. Therefore, option D is the correct answer.

13. B, C - Topic 101.2

The Linux kernel accepts many boot parameters at the moment it is started. One of these is **single**, which is used to boot the system in single-user mode for rescue operations. Therefore, option B is the correct answer. You can also specify **s** or **1** instead of **single** to accomplish the same task (runlevel 1 matches single user mode), making also option C correct. For completeness, the **debug** parameter is used to enable kernel debugging, while the **single-mode** and **single-user** parameters are not valid.

14. C - Topic 103.6

The **nice** command is used to run a program with an adjusted niceness. If no adjustment value is specified, the **nice** command uses 10 as a default. Therefore, option C is the correct answer.

15. A, C - Topic 104.3

The **blkid** command is used to display information about available block devices, displaying attributes such as the universally unique identifier (UUID), the file system type (TYPE) and the volume label (LABEL). This makes option A the correct answer. The **lsblk** command is used to list information about the specified block devices and the output columns to print (NAME, UUID, FSTYPE, LABEL) are indicated through the -o (--output) option. Therefore, also option C is correct. For completeness, options B and E specify invalid commands, while option D gives a format error.

16. /proc/ioports - Topic 101.1

The **/proc/ioports** file contains a list of currently registered Input-Output port regions that are in use on the system. Other important files that you can find under the **/proc** tree are: **/proc/interrupts** that lists what IRQs are being used for different purposes in the system and **/proc/dma** that holds information about DMA channels in use.

17. B - Topic 103.7

The **grep** command is used to print lines matching a pattern. The -E (--extended-regexp) option tells **grep** to interpret the specified pattern as an extended regular expression so that you don't need to escape special characters such as curly brackets. The **[aeiou]** expression matches a single character that is contained within the square brackets (the vowels **a**, **e**, **i**, **o** or **u**) and the **{min,}** expression specifies that the preceding item is matched **min** or more times. Therefore, the command specified in the question finds any line in the file with two or more vowels in a row, making option B the correct answer.

18.C - Topic 103.6

The **renice** command is used to alter the scheduling priority of one or more running processes, while the **nice** command is used to run a program with modified scheduling priority. These two commands are distinct and achieve different goals, making option A the incorrect answer. Option D describes the **nice** command and is therefore incorrect. The **renice** command can be used by ordinary users, but they can only give their processes a lower scheduling priority. In fact, only users with root privileges can increase a process priority. This makes option C correct and option B incorrect.

19.D - Topic 102.2

The **grub-install** command is used to install GRUB Legacy to a device. With the **--root-directory=DIR** option, the command installs a GRUB image under the directory **DIR** instead of the root directory. This makes option D the correct answer. Options A, B and C contain invalid options for **grub-install** and are therefore incorrect.

20.A, E - Topic 104.3

The fourth field in the **/etc/fstab** file describes the mount options associated with the filesystem. The **defaults** option that you can specify includes the following options: **rw** (to mount the filesystem read/write), **suid** (to allow SUID or SGID bits to take effect), **dev** (to interpret character or block special devices on the filesystem), **exec** (to permit the execution of binaries), **auto** (to mount the filesystem at boot time or when root types the **mount -a** command), **nouser** (to do not allow an ordinary user to mount the filesystem) and **async** (all I/O to the filesystem should be done asynchronously). Therefore, options A and E are the correct answers. For completeness, the **ro** option is used to mount the filesystem read-only, the **user** option is used to allow ordinary users to mount the filesystem so that only the user who mounted the filesystem could unmount it, and the **users** option is used to allow ordinary users to mount the filesystem so that any user could unmount the filesystem once it's been mounted.

21. A - Topic 101.2

If you want to modify kernel parameters or add new ones, when the GRUB Legacy menu shows up you must select and edit (pressing the **e** key) the entry that you want to modify and then locate and edit the **kernel** line. For example, on this line you can add the parameters to boot in single-user mode, to specify an alternate root filesystem to boot from, to enable kernel debugging, to disable all log messages and so on. Therefore, option A is the correct answer.

22. C - Topic 101.2

The initial RAM disk (initrd) is an initial root filesystem that is mounted during the system boot. It contains drivers and executables and it provides support to the kernel for the real filesystem mounting, after which it is subsequently unmounted. So the initial RAM disk allows system startup occurring in two phases, where the kernel comes up with a minimum set of compiled-in drivers, and where additional modules are loaded from initrd. This makes option C the correct answer.

23. B - Topic 101.3

The **shutdown** command is used to bring the system down in a secure way, notifying all logged-in users that the system is going down. The -r option of this command is used to reboot after shutdown. It is possible to shut the system down immediately or after a delay, specifying a time argument. It can be an absolute time in the format **hh:mm**, where **hh** is the hour (one or two digits) and **mm** is the minute of the hour (in two digits) or it can be in the format **+m**, where **m** is the number of minutes to wait. The word **now** is an alias for **+0**. An optional waring message can be also specified to give logged-in users more detailed information about the shutdown. This makes option B the correct answer. Option A is used to reboot the system in one minute and is therefore incorrect. The **shutdown** command has not the -m or --messages options and so options C and D are the incorrect answers.

24.C - Topic 103.1

The bash built-in **set** command is used to change the values of shell options and to display the values of shell variables. The -o option of this command is used to set a specific option. In particular, the **-o vi** option specifies bash to use a vi-style command line editing interface, while **-o emacs** option specifies bash to use an emacs-style command line editing interface. This makes option C the correct answer. Options A and B try to set invalid options and are therefore incorrect. The **set** command has not the --disable and --enable options, making options D and E the incorrect answer.

25.B - Topic 102.4

On a Debian-derived GNU/Linux system **apt-get** is the command-line tool for handling packages. It has several subcommands such as **clean** that is used to clear out the local repository of retrieved package files and **autoclean** that is similar to **clean**, but only removes package files that can no longer be downloaded and are largely useless. Therefore, option B is the correct answer, while option A is incorrect. On Debian-based systems **apt-cache** performs a variety of operations on APT's package cache, but it has not the **clean** or **autoclean** subcommands, making options C and D incorrect.

26.C, D - Topic 103.7

The **grep** command (option B) is used to print the lines of one or more files matching a pattern. The **egrep** (option D) and **grep -E** (option C) commands are used to search for a pattern inside one or more files using extended regular expressions. The **fgrep** and **grep -F** (option E) commands are used to search for fixed-character strings in one or more files so that the string is interpreted literally and regular expressions cannot be used. The **rgrep** (option A) and **grep -r** commands are used to recursively find files that match the specified criteria string. Therefore, options C and D are the correct answers.

27.A - Topic 103.3

The **rm** command is used to remove files and directories. By default, it does not remove directories, but you can use the -r (or -R or --recursive) option to remove the specified directories and their contents recursively. This makes option A the correct answer. Option B removes the **foo** file (if it exists), while option C removes the contents of the **foo** directory recursively, but not the directory itself and its hidden files. Therefore, these two options are incorrect. The **rmdir** command is used to remove empty directories and it has not a -r option, making options D and E the incorrect answers.

28.B - Topic 102.5

Zypper is a command line package manager used for installing, updating and removing packages as well as for managing repositories. If you want to enable or disable a specified **zypper repository**, you can use the **zypper modifyrepo** (or **zypper mr**) command with the -e or -d option, respectively. Therefore, option B is the correct answer. The **zypper removerepo** (or **zypper rr**) command is used to remove a specified repository and it has not a --disable option, making options A and D the incorrect answers. Option C contains an invalid **zypper** subcommand and is therefore incorrect.

29.B - Topic 103.3

The **ls** command is used to list directory contents and the -l option of this command specifies to use a long listing format. The command in the question uses the wildcard support that is built into the bash shell. In particular, **[a-z]** means matching any single character enclosed by the brackets and so any lowercase character from **a** to **z**. Therefore, the command lists all four-character files beginning by three lowercase characters followed by the digit 1 in the specified directory (**/foobar**), making option B the correct answer.

30.A - Topic 104.1

Common type codes of MBR partitions are: **0x82** (option A), which refers to a Linux swap partition, **0x83** (option B), which refers to a Linux native filesystem,

0x05 (option C), which refers to an old type of extended partition and **0x0f** (option D), which refers to a newer type of extended partition. Therefore, option A is the correct answer.

31. B, E - Topic 104.7

The **find** command is used to search for files in a directory hierarchy. It can be used to perform sophisticated searches, finding files by name, size, type and so on. The **locate** command is used to find files by name and so it performs less complex searches then **find**, making option A the incorrect answer. Both commands are not deprecated and so options C and D are incorrect. The **locate** command works from a database that can be updated through the **updatedb** command. So, if the database is not updated, **locate** may not find recent files or it may return names of files that no longer exist. Therefore, option B is the correct answer. Since **locate** works from a database, it is usually much faster then **find,** making also option E correct.

32. D - Topic 103.5

Option D describes the behavior of the **jobs** command correctly: in fact, typing **jobs** on the command line, you obtain the list of jobs associated with your terminal and their job numbers (the -l option lists also the PIDs of the jobs). So the **jobs** command does not display neither the jobs of all terminals nor the jobs of the parent shell, making options B and C incorrect. Option A describes the effect of the **top** command and is therefore incorrect.

33. A - Topic 104.1

The **gdisk** command with the -l option is used to list partitions for GPT formatted disks, making option A the correct answer. Option C simply displays the contents of the **/etc/fstab** file (that contains the list of the filesystems that the system can mount) and is therefore incorrect. The **gptable** and **gptdisk** commands are not valid and so options B and D are the incorrect answers.

34. B, D - Topic 104.6

A symbolic link is a special file that points to a directory or to another file by name. In order to create a symbolic link, you can use the **ln** command with the -s (--symbolic) option or the **cp** command with the -s (--symbolic-link) option. Therefore, options B and D are the correct answers. The **ln** command and the **cp** command with the -l (--link) option are used to create hard links, making options E and C incorrect. Option A contains an invalid command and is therefore incorrect.

35. B - Topic 103.3

The **mv** command is used to move or rename files. The file you have created and you want to rename contains a special character (\) and so you need to escape it with a backslash or protect it with single quotes. In order to access to the home directory of the **foobar** user, you can use the **~foobar** syntax. In fact, the shell replaces it with the home directory of **foobar**, transparently, and passes that in its place. Therefore, option B is the correct answer.

36. C - Topic 103.4

In redirections the **<** operator is used to redirect the standard input from a specified file. So the **foobar** command gets its input from the **foo** file, making option C the correct answer. Options A, B and D describe the effect of the **foo >foobar**, **foobar > foo** and **foo < foobar** commands, respectively, and are therefore incorrect.

37. 002 - Topic 104.5

The **umask** command can be used to set the file mode creation mask. This command takes an octal value as argument and, if fewer than four digits are entered, leading zeros are assumed. In Linux, the default permissions are 666 for a regular file, and 777 for a directory. So the permissions of newly created files (ordinary files or directories) are given by "subtracting" the umask value from the default permissions. It's not really subtraction (technically is a little bit complicated), but thinking the operation as a subtraction can help new Linux users to calculate the exact resulting permissions of new files. Therefore, if you want to have default permissions of 664 (rw-rw-r--) for new files and 775 (rwxrwxr-x) for new directories you should set the umask value to 002.

38. C - Topic 104.5

The sticky bit is primarily used on shared directories, such as **/tmp**, where users can create their files, read and execute files owned by other users and remove only their own files. The sticky bit allows the files in the directory where it is set to be deleted only by their owners, the directory' s owner and root. Therefore, option C is the correct answer.

39. D - Topic 104.2

The **tune2fs** command is used to adjust tunable filesystem parameters on **ext2**, **ext3** and **ext4** filesystems. In particular, the -j option of this command is used to add an **ext3** journal to the **ext2** filesystem, making option D the correct answer. For completeness, the **dumpe2fs** command is used to print the superblock and blocks group information for the filesystem present on the specified device (and it has not a -E option), the **e2fsck** command is used to check the **ext2**, **ext3**, **ext4** family of filesystems (the -E option of this command is used to set extended options) and the **conv2ext3** command is not valid.

40. D - Topic 103.3

The **tar** command is used to create an archive file and to restore files from such an archive. The archive in the question has been compressed with the **bzip2** compression program and so it has the **.tar.bz2** extension. If you want to extract files from this compressed archive, you can use the **tar** command with the -xjvf options. In fact, the -x option extracts files from the specified archive, the -j option filters the archive through **bzip2**, the -f option specifies file input, rather than stdin and the -v option lists files processed verbosely. Alternatively, you can pipe the **bzcat** command to **tar** with the -xvf options. This makes option D the correct answer. The **bzcat** command is used to only view the contents of a file compressed with the **bzip2** compression program without uncompressing it, the **tar** command with the -tvf options is used to list the contents of a tar archive file and the **tar** command with the -xzvf options is used to extract files from an archive compressed with **gzip**. Therefore, options A, B and C are incorrect. The command in option E achieves the same goal as the one specified in option C and so it is not the right command to use.

41. C - Topic 102.3

Option C contains the exact procedure that a user must follow to test an experimental version of a custom library and is therefore the correct answer. In fact, the additional directories containing the new library files must be added to the list specified by the environment variable named **LD_LIBRARY_PATH**.

42. B - Topic 104.2

The **df** command is used to display the amount of disk space available on the filesystems that contain the files specified as arguments on the command line. If no file is given, it shows the space available (and thus used) on all currently mounted filesystems. Therefore, option B is the correct answer. The **free** command is used to display the amount of free and used memory in the system, while the **du** command is used to summarize disk usage of each specified file, recursively for directories. This makes options C and A incorrect. Option D contains an invalid command and is therefore incorrect.

43. B - Topic 103.4

Option B describes the effect of the command exactly and is therefore the correct answer. In fact, the pipe (|) operator concatenates the **foobar** and **barfoo** commands so that the output of **foobar** is used as input of **barfoo** that then redirects (>) its output to the **bar** file.

44. B - Topic 102.1

The MBR partitioning system uses up to four primary partitions, numbered from one to four, one of which can be an extended partition. The extended partition is a special type of primary partition that contains logical partitions that are numbered five and up. Therefore, **/dev/sda5** is the first logical partition on the first SCSI disk, making option B the correct answer.

45. A - Topic 102.5

Yum is an interactive, rpm based package manager. It has several subcommands such as **whatprovides** (or **provides**) that is used to find out which packages provide the specified feature, **info** that is used to display information about the specified package and **deplist** that is used to produce a list of all dependencies of the given package. This makes option A correct and options B and C incorrect. Option D contains an invalid **yum** subcommand and is therefore incorrect.

46. D - Topic 103.4

The **xargs** command is used to build and execute command lines from standard input. In particular, it reads items from the standard input, delimited by blanks or newlines, and executes a command (by default **echo**) one or more times with any initial-arguments followed by the items read from standard input. It is often used with the **find** command to operate on files that match specified attributes. So, in order to accomplish the task of the question, you can use the **find** command that searches for regular files (**-type f**) belonging to the user with uid 1001 (**-user 1001**) in the root directory (**/**) and then you can pipe the results to **xargs**, which runs the **rm -f** command on each file and removes them. Therefore, option D is the correct answer.

47. C - Topic 101.3

The **systemctl** command is used to control the Systemd system and service manager. It has several subcommands such as **start** that is used to activate one or more units specified on the command line and **enable** that is used to enable one or more units or unit instances, creating a set of symbolic links so that, for example, a specific unit is automatically started on boot or when a particular kind of hardware is plugged in. This makes option C correct and option B incorrect. Options A and D contain invalid **systemctl** subcommands and are therefore incorrect.

48. lspci - Topic 101.1

The **lspci** command is used to obtain information about PCI devices. By default, it shows a brief list of devices, but you can request more verbose output using the -v, -vv or -vvv options.

49. B - Topic 102.2

The name of the main configuration file for GRUB Legacy is normally **/boot/grub/grub.conf** or **/boot/grub/menu.lst**, while the name of the main configuration file for GRUB 2 is normally **/boot/grub/grub.cfg**. Therefore, option B is the correct answer.

50. B - Topic 103.8

Using the **vi** editor, you can switch in command mode by pressing the ESC key. This makes options C and D incorrect. Once entered in command mode, you can type a series of commands such as **dd** to delete the entire current line and **Ndd** (or **dNd**) to delete N lines, beginning with the current line. So option B enters in command mode and deletes the current line and the next ten lines and is the correct answer. Option A enters in command mode and copies the current line and the next ten lines into the buffer, while option E enters in command mode and deletes eleven characters in total, starting with the character under the cursor. Therefore, these two options are incorrect.

51. D - Topic 103.1

The **env** command is used to print a list of the current environment variables or to run another program in a custom environment. Therefore, option D is the correct answer.

52. B - Topic 102.1

The **/lib** directory contains essential shared libraries and kernel modules and should never be placed on a separate partition because it is vital for the boot process. Instead, the **/home**, **/tmp** and **/usr** directories are commonly split off into separate partitions. The **/home** directory holds user data files and, putting it on a separate partition, will preserve users' data files during system upgrades or in case of servers' re-installation. It can be a very large partition on systems with many users or if users store large data files as happens for file servers. The **/tmp** directory holds temporary files created by programs and users and in some distributions is periodically cleaned out by specific routines, sometimes at bootup. The **/usr** directory contains most program and data files, can be shared with other Linux systems and is mounted read-only. Based on these considerations, option B is the correct answer.

53.A - Topic 102.4

On a Debian-derived GNU/Linux system **apt-get** is the command-line tool for handling packages. It has several subcommands such as **update** that is used to re-synchronize the package index files from their sources, **upgrade** that is used to install the newest versions of all packages currently installed on the system, (based on locally stored information about available packages) and **dist-upgrade** that is used to perform the function of **upgrade**, also handling intelligently the dependencies with new versions of packages. This makes option A correct and option B incorrect. The **distribution-upgrade** subcommand is not valid and therefore option E is incorrect. On Debian-based systems **apt-cache** performs a variety of operations on APT's package cache, but it has not the **update** or **upgrade** subcommands, making options C and D the incorrect answers.

54.D - Topic 103.7

The **grep** command is used to print the lines of one or more files matching a pattern. The -r (or -R or --recursive) option is used to recursively find files under the specified directory that match the criteria string. This is equivalent to the **-d recurse** (or --directories=recurse) option. The -E option is used to search for a pattern inside one or more files using extended regular expressions without the need of escaping some special characters. Therefore, option D is the correct answer since it uses the -r option and escapes the special characters (round brackets and pipe). For completeness, option B does not escape any special characters and options A and C use extended regular expressions, but they escape the special characters.

55. A - Topic 104.6

A symbolic link is a special file that points to a directory or to another file by name. Therefore, symbolic links can span across different filesystems, making option A the correct answer. You can create symbolic links for files and directories and when you delete the original file the symbolic link become a broken link. Therefore, options C and D are incorrect. Option B describes hard links and so it is the incorrect answer.

56. D - Topic 102.6

A clone is a new virtual machine that is created by copying an existing virtual machine. It is independent of the original virtual machine and so any changes to the original virtual machine will not appear in the clone and any changes to the clone will not appear in the original virtual machine, making option C the incorrect answer. The cloned virtual machine has the same settings, software and contents of the original virtual machine; therefore, you need to customize your guest operating system changing some of the properties of the clone, such as the computer name and the networking settings. This prevents from conflicts that might occur if you deploy virtual machines with identical settings, such as duplicate computer names or IP addresses. This makes option D correct and option B incorrect. If you want to clone frequently a virtual machine, you can convert it in a template. In fact, a template is a master copy of a virtual machine that can be used to create many clones. So you can create a clone from a template or you can clone directly from an existing virtual machine. Therefore, it is not necessary to convert the original virtual machine in a template for cloning it and option A is incorrect.

57. B - Topic 103.8

Using the **vi** editor in command mode, you can execute an external command by typing **:!** followed by the command you want to run. Therefore, if you type **:!ls** the external command **ls** will be executed so that you can see what files are present in your current working directory. This makes option B the correct answer.

58. B, C - Topic 103.2

The **cat** command is used to concatenate files, or standard input, to standard output. By default, this command does not number output lines and therefore option D is incorrect. The -n (--number) option is used to number all output lines, while the -b (--number-nonblank) option is used to number non-empty output lines. This makes option C correct and option A incorrect. The **nl** command is used to write one or more specified files to standard output, with line numbers added. You can specify body, header and footer style with the -b, -h and -f options. The most common style values are: **a** to number all lines, **t** to number only non-empty lines and **n** to number no lines. Therefore, also option B is the correct answer, while option E is incorrect.

59. D - Topic 103.5

The **pgrep** command looks up processes and lists the PIDs that match the specified selection criteria. You can search for processes based on name and other attributes (for example usernames, user IDs, group IDs) and matching regular expressions. All the criteria have to match. The **pkill** command sends a specified signal to processes and uses the same selection criteria of **pgrep**. This makes option D the correct answer. The other options contain combinations of commands that cannot be used to accomplish the tasks specified in the question and are therefore incorrect. In particular, the **jobs** command is used to find out what jobs are running in the current shell, the **kill** command is used to send a signal to processes based on PIDs, the **killall** command is used to kill processes by name and the **watch** command is used to execute a program periodically, showing full-screen output.

60. D - Topic 102.5

On a RPM-based distribution it may be sometimes useful to extract data from a RPM package without installing it. The **rpm2cpio** command is used to convert a .**rpm** file, specified as a single argument, to a **cpio archive** on standard output. Then you can use the **cpio** command to retrieve individual files. You can also link these two commands together using a pipe as stated in option D that is therefore the correct answer. The final effect of the command is to extract the files in the specified archive in the current working directory. The **rpm** command has not the --extract and --extract-archive2tar options this makes options A and B incorrect. The command in option C is not valid and so this option is the incorrect answer.